GHOST WHISPERS

Neil D'Silva is an accomplished author, best known for his works in the horror genre, such as *Maya's New Husband*, *Yakshini*, *Pishacha*, *Sapna's Bad Connection*, and *Devputra*.

Neil has played a key role in shaping the horror literature landscape in India. He has served as president of the Indian chapter of the Horror Writers Association and was the Jury Chair for a year in the short stories category for the Bram Stoker® Awards. He has also judged other notable literary competitions, including the 'Wattpad India Awards'.

A passionate advocate for India's folklore and paranormal horror literature, Neil is a sought-after speaker who has delivered talks on the TEDx platform and featured on leading podcasts such as *The Ranveer Show*, *Astro Arun Pandit Show* and Khooni Monday's *Ankhon Dekhi*, among others.

He is also a mentor with the Scholastic Writers Academy, where he guides emerging writers in honing their craft and building their voices in fiction.

Neil has adapted several of his novels for the screen and has provided the original story for an upcoming fantasy-horror web series on an OTT platform.

Sarbajeet Mohanty, with over thirteen years of experience in paranormal investigations, is a leading expert committed to uncovering the mysteries of the supernatural. He is the co-founder of the Parapsychology and Investigations Research Society (PAIRS) and Ghost Encounters India, through which he has conducted groundbreaking investigations across the globe.

Sarbajeet also co-hosted MTV Dark Scroll alongside actor Amit Sadh and Pooja Vijay, bringing the world of the unseen to a mainstream audience. Known for his fearless explorations and scientific approach, he has earned recognition as one of India's most respected voices in the paranormal field.

GHOST WHISPERS

SPINE-CHILLING STORIES OF PARANORMAL INVESTIGATIONS

NEIL D'SILVA
AND
SARBAJEET MOHANTY

RUPA

Published by
Rupa Publications India Pvt. Ltd 2025
161-B/4, Gulmohar House,
Yusuf Sarai Community Centre,
New Delhi 110049

Sales centres:
Bengaluru Chennai
Hyderabad Kolkata Mumbai

This book is based on true incidents but the authors have changed the names, characters and places to protect the privacy of individuals. The publisher and the authors are in no way liable or responsible for any similarity that the characters or events in the book may bear with any person or for any loss or incidental or consequential damages caused to any person or entity, or alleged to have been caused, directly or indirectly, by the contents of the book. The views and opinions expressed in this book are the authors' own and the publishers are not in any way liable for the same.

P-ISBN: 978-93-7003-549-2
E-ISBN: 978-93-7003-585-0

Second impression 2025

10 9 8 7 6 5 4 3 2

CONTENTS

INTRODUCTION

On a Long Summer's Night...

Some things are just meant to be.

It was a sultry March evening in 2018 when Suhail Mathur, my literary agent, sent me a message. Writers will understand how valuable such unexpected messages from their agents are, so I understandably stopped whatever it was that I was doing and tapped on the notification. I was surprised to find an image; it was a digital poster of a meetup to be held in Bandra, a suburb of Mumbai. The headline screamed: 'Paranormal Meetup in Mumbai'. It was organized by a group called PAIRS (Parapsychology and Investigations Research Society), which I had never heard of. Suhail suggested that we attend the meetup together to see if we could connect with the speakers. He had a good feeling about the whole thing, and soon the good vibes caught on to me.

The meetup was organized at a bungalow in Bandra West. It was in a somewhat desolate neighbourhood within the suburb, away from the hubbub of traffic on the main roads. The bungalow itself fit the description of a haunted location. Old and discreet, it had a main hall where a large wooden table was set up for the attendees to sit around, and two ladders leading to an upper floor which was out of bounds for the visitors. At the far end of the hall were a kitchen and the bathrooms. This area was not directly visible from the sitting area and, plunged in darkness, added to the creepy vibe of the entire setup.

Then the speakers came in. And for the first time, I met the duo with whom I would soon strike a strong friendship. They were the co-founders of PAIRS—paranormal investigator Sarbajeet Mohanty and psychic expert Pooja Vijay. My first impression of them was: 'Oh, they're really young!' And they were warm and affable, not quite the image of a sombre paranormal investigator that most of us generally have.

Then the meetup began. More people had joined in. Among them were famous horror film directors, businessmen and healing experts. Sarbajeet and Pooja guided the audience to share their paranormal experiences. As people began to speak, they drew on their reserves of personal horror stories, and soon we were all engulfed in an atmosphere that none of us would forget. These stories were interspersed with Sarbajeet and Pooja's analyses of them. It was soon clear to me that there was something unique about this duo. While they were familiar with the paranormal terminology that applied to both the Indian and Western worlds, they were not blind followers of these beliefs. They were rational people who questioned. They debunked some of the horror stories with logical reasoning. And they spoke of things such as past-life regression, sleep paralysis, near-death experiences, residual hauntings, electronic voice phenomena and many more.

It didn't take long for me to understand that PAIRS wasn't just a group of superficial hobbyists; they knew and meant business.

Then things got rolling. At the end of the meeting, Suhail and I met Sarbajeet and Pooja and talked to them about an idea we had discussed before the meetup—chronicling their knowledge in a book. We even had a concept ready. The book would blend Indian and Western paranormal knowledge, without adopting either a blindly credulous or a staunchly sceptical stance. Reasoning and research would be the core of this book.

It barely took Sarbajeet ten minutes to give his nod!

And so began the journey of *Ghost Whispers*, a book we worked on for the next year and a half, and which we now present to you.

It is apt to speak about the kind of work PAIRS does before diving into their world. Founded in 2016, PAIRS is an organization that deals with paranormal investigations at reportedly haunted locations. They usually get their cases via calls from clients across the country, and they also seek out locations which have a reputation of being haunted and investigate them on their own. Their investigations have taken them to some of the most haunted locations in the country, including the abandoned village of Kuldhara, the severely tragic site of Lambi Dehar mines, a famous historical battlefield in Odisha, and many others. Having cultivated a formidable expertise from conducting around a hundred investigations, and hosting television shows (starting with *Mana Ke Na Mana* on an Odia television channel to *Dark Scroll* on MTV India in 2024), PAIRS has become a force to reckon with on the Indian paranormal scene.

Sarbajeet hails from Bhubaneswar in Odisha. His life transformed in his early years when he had to fight his claustrophobia and fear of darkness. At the age of 15, Sarbajeet warded off his mental demons with grit and determination. He told himself that there was nothing to be afraid of in the dark. This thought expanded his horizons. At this time, he also began to develop a particular sensitivity to his surroundings. He was no longer afraid of the dark. Instead, he could now feel a special connection with it. He found that he could understand positive and negative energies which often dictated the makeup of a place or a person. This sent him on a voyage of self-discovery and he landed in Mumbai.

One of the first things he did was to try to learn whatever he could from the existing sources of the paranormal sciences. He began by reading all the relevant books he could catch hold of and then extensively studied various topics that fall under the paranormal domain, especially demonology. He read up on several cases from the past and explored the unexplained mysteries of the present. At the age of 17, trained and authorized by demonologists certified to perform exorcisms, he himself became the youngest demonologist in the world.

In 2016, he co-founded PAIRS with Pooja Vijay whom he had met on a paranormal chat group. The two bonded immediately and discovered that they had a shared intention to dispel the myths surrounding the paranormal sciences. They soon established the company and were roped in to anchor the TV show, *Mana Ke Na Mana*. A modicum of fame came their way when celebrities and spiritual gurus began to reach out to them to both lend them their support and know more about their line of work. PAIRS was now well on the path that its founders had envisioned.

PAIRS has now diversified into various allied activities. They organize past life regressions and meditation courses. They train novices in this field. Several of the current team members started out as trainee paranormal investigators with PAIRS. Perhaps one of the biggest steps in their career is the inception of a festival called ScareCon, billed as Asia's largest paranormal convention.

They are arguably the most prolific paranormal investigation team in the country at present, with their many contributions to the domain. Apart from the activities mentioned above, they conduct Ghost Encounters tours to various locations in the country, guiding enthusiasts to experience paranormal phenomena up close (and debunk false theories). They also have a highly active YouTube channel with close to 2.5 lakh subscribers at the time of writing this (2025).

Our humble work, *Ghost Whispers*, is another major milestone in PAIRS' journey. More than that, it is a document of their case files and an eye-opener for anyone interested in learning about the paranormal world in a way that has not been explained before.

I am Neil D'Silva, writer of the bizarre and mysterious, and co-author of *Ghost Whispers*, along with Sarbajeet Mohanty. The pages that lie ahead of you bear my words and my voice, but the stories are of Sarbajeet Mohanty and his colleagues at PAIRS. We especially thank Pooja Vijay, noted psychic and co-founder of PAIRS, for lending her thoughts and inputs on some of the stories in the book.

But these are not just stories. Backing them up are our theories and explanations that attempt to shed light on many of the unknown phenomena that this universe holds for us, and yet keeps them hidden from our ordinary eyes.

We hope you enjoy this book.

—Neil D'Silva

A LONG NIGHT WITH GHOSTS

Electronic Voice Phenomenon

The communication of the dead is tongued with fire beyond the language of the living.

—T.S. Eliot

In early 2019, Sarbajeet Mohanty was contacted by the team of horror filmmaker Vikram Bhatt with an interesting request. Bhatt had just finished shooting his film *Ghost*, and wanted to give the media some insight into the real haunted world as part of his promotional campaign for the film. The film team approached the Parapsychology and Investigations Research Society (PAIRS) with a request to organize a tour of a well-known haunted location where people could see how a paranormal investigation is conducted and get closer to finding out if ghosts really exist.

Sarbajeet and his partner, clairvoyant Pooja Vijay, began scouting for haunted locations where Bhatt's team and some chosen media persons could be led through an investigation. Their research revealed dozens of such places. It was truly astounding how many places in the heart of the bustling Mumbai metropolitan region were considered to be abodes of ghosts and spirits. After deliberating for three days, they zeroed in on a popular fort on the outskirts of the city.

The fort perfectly fitted the bill. Built 340 years ago, the fort had been attacked several times by three different foreign invaders. Due to its location on the city's coastline, it was also an easy target for pirates who pillaged and plundered it on multiple occasions. There are no existing records of these conquests and invasions, but it is believed that the number of brutal deaths that took place in the ramparts of the fort might have numbered in the thousands.

Locals maintain that many of these entities still haunt the premises. They are still lurking around, looking for something—perhaps an unfulfilled life? As the sun sets, the few people in the vicinity make a hasty departure, lending the whole area a desolate look. Many have reported sightings of apparitions walking or standing guard on the ramparts of the fort, as they must have done centuries ago.

Permission was sought to lead an investigation of the fort and it was duly granted by the concerned authorities. However, there was a rider—the fort could not be named. All the parties involved accepted this condition and the preliminary investigation began.

The night before the filmmaker's team and the media persons were to visit the fort, Sarbajeet and Pooja conducted a recce of the location with a handful of their team members. That night was a precursor to the events that were to follow.

The moment they reached the location, Pooja, who is

believed to have enhanced psychic powers, experienced a feeling of being trapped by a negative energy. She describes it as a 'deeply unsettling feeling imbued with sorrow', but she couldn't say exactly where this aura was emanating from. They decided to enter the fort to find out more.

The fort had a domed arch at the entrance and several vaulted corridors leading into the inner rooms. These rooms encircled a central pentagonal hall, which might have been the assembly area when the site was inhabited. As they walked along this corridor, Sarbajeet kept a close watch on Pooja. The deeper they went, the stronger was the aura of negativity that Pooja felt, until they came to an area downstairs that had a row of rooms. These rooms were smaller and looked like barracks for the soldiers who lived in the fort. Here, Pooja lost control of herself. It was like a headrush, the feeling of blood flowing suddenly into her head, and if Sarbajeet hadn't held her, she might have crashed on the floor. He made her sit on one of the cleaner window ledges, and waited for her breath to normalize.

Sarbajeet realized that she just had a vision of the past. He made her sit down on a stone bench, and she described what she had seen, 'This place was once a prison. There are hundreds of souls here, but they are trapped. They appear to me like the souls of prisoners who wail and scream, but are unable to get out of their cells.'

Intrigued but worried about Pooja's condition, Sarbajeet asked, 'Why are they not able to come out?'

'Because…' Pooja said, choosing her words cautiously, 'They still believe they are in prison. These prisoners were tortured so badly during the last days of their lives that they didn't even realize it when they died.'

'Can you hear their voices?' Sarbajeet gently prodded.

'Yes, I can.'

Shocked by this revelation, the team vacated the fort, now better prepared to return the following day with the media persons. The voices were what they wanted. With the right equipment, they could get the evidence they needed.

The next day, the filmmaker arrived at the fort with fifteen media persons. Sarbajeet and Pooja explained to the group what they were about to get into.

'This place is teeming with spirits,' Sarbajeet said. 'There are good and bad spirits, but most of them are just confused spirits.'

'Can you elaborate on that?' asked a young reporter from the media.

'Absolutely,' said Sarbajeet. 'Our horror movies and shows often depict ghosts as evil. They are shown as villains or antagonists. But the truth is that not all spirits are bad. Some of them are just stuck in this plane and want to find deliverance. The default tendency of a spirit is not to do us harm. Most of the spirit-related incidents happen because the humans involved acted in hazardous ways due to their fright. Hence, I ask you, stay cool and composed. Even if we encounter something here tonight, I don't want anything untoward to happen.'

'That's an interesting perspective on ghosts,' another media person said.

'We need to be respectful of them,' Sarbajeet added, 'and the most important thing—there is absolutely no reason to be afraid.'

With great apprehension, the group was led into the more confined parts of the fort. This was a never-before-done kind of investigation, and there was no clue as to what was going to unfold in these confines.

The path had already been decided. They would walk from the entrance to the general area of the prison cells along the vaulted corridors. They would save the prison cells for the end, and only enter them if the group felt brave enough to do so.

It was after 8.00 p.m., and since the area was away from the main city, the darkness was absolute. Apart from the lights of the phones and other devices the people had with them, there was no illumination. 'I was aware that the changed light conditions would make the spirits uncomfortable and they could act in unpredictable ways,' Sarbajeet said. 'But it was a chance we had to take, albeit cautiously.'

The group moved forward. Everyone had already been warned to maintain absolute silence, as this was the only way to capture any unexpected sounds. But more importantly, they did not want to aggravate the spirits too much.

Sarbajeet had a strange device with him, which he held aloft, and routinely observed. 'What does this device do?' asked the director.

Sarbajeet said, 'This is a K2 meter, also known as a ghost meter or EMF meter. It detects electromagnetic frequency. It is believed that ghosts alter the EMF of their surroundings. So when this device lights up, we know something is different.'

'But don't electrical wires and mobile phones trigger

the device as well?' asked a media person.

"Yes. There are five lights on my device. They are in order of increasing EMF. Under normal conditions, one light is always on due to the electromagnetic fields around us. But anything beyond that is not considered normal.'

'What do normal conditions mean?' asked the reporter.

'It's like your phones or tablets,' Sarbajeet said. 'Such devices trigger the device too. If the LEDs are constantly glowing, don't flinch or blink, it means the signal is coming from a human-originated source like these electronic devices. But if they start to blink or even if more than one light starts blinking, we can assume that something is odd.'

They walked ahead in a single group, with Sarbajeet and Pooja leading the way. Both of them now had K2 meters. As they walked along a corridor, all five lights on Sarbajeet's meter lit up. He stood absolutely still, holding the device aloft. A videographer continued to film the moment. Making a gesture to the party to remain silent, Sarbajeet said, 'Hello, is anyone here?'

The device flashed its second light, as if in assent!

The filmmaker repeated the question, and a similar response was obtained.

While the media persons gasped at what they saw before them, Sarbajeet led them deeper into the corridor. They could now see the prison area. Still standing in the corridor, Sarbajeet asked everyone to wait, and said, 'Hello, we are a group of people here. If there is anyone here, please reply.'

In the presence of about 20 people, the devices held by the crew suddenly began to behave irrationally. Sarbajeet's

K2 meter was already blinking, but now the other EMF meter that was in Pooja's hand began to report a high-level response. Indeed, the electromagnetic frequency at the spot was irrationally high, which is believed to be the first indicator of a ghostly presence.

Just then, an intern of the PAIRS team who was operating the camera drew the attention of the group to a significant drop in temperature at the spot where he was standing. The infrared thermometer he was carrying had dropped from 29 degrees Celsius to 27.9 degrees Celsius. There was also an unmistakable damp stench in the air.

Bhatt took the opportunity to speak to those present. 'We know someone is here,' he said. 'If you are here, could you reply with a "yes"? Please indicate it by making the K2 meter blink only once.'[1]

Almost as if on cue, that's exactly what happened.

The group was now dead silent, witnessing these incredible events. Then Sarbajeet took out another device and told the group, 'Guys, this is a PSB7 box. It is a special device for listening to spirit communication.'

'How does it work?' Bhatt asked, fascinated.

'It goes like this. This device can basically scan all radio frequencies, and it can do that in forward or reverse order. When it scans, it produces white noise. The spirits

---

[1]A question arose during this investigation as to what language may be used to communicate with the spirits. The theory behind this is spirits operate at a higher level of consciousness than humans. Their intellect transcends language. Normally, if a spirit is communicative, it will respond to any language. However, paranormal investigators do try different languages and prefer local languages as it might make the process simpler and more relatable.

use this white noise to communicate with us. If we are attentive, we will be able to make out words in the white noise,' Sarbajeet explained.

'But what if it's just a word floating in the air? I mean, a word spoken on one of the usual radio wavelengths?' asked one of the media persons.

'That's why we have the reverse frequency scanning option,' Sarbajeet explained. 'This way we can be sure that the word or phrase we hear, if we hear it, is not of human origin.'

People now began to look at the PSB7 device, also known as the spirit box, with awe. And quite rightly so, as this device enabled paranormal investigators to communicate with the other side.

Could spirits really talk to us in a human voice that we could understand? This was the question in many of their minds. They were about to find out shortly.

The question was interrupted by a noise from the device. It was only a single, quickly uttered syllable. Bhatt, who was now very excited, told Sarbajeet, 'Play that again. What was that?'

The recording was played again. It was a human male voice, a deep baritone, and sounded like *'Hain*?'

'It sounds like a question, maybe in Hindi,' Bhatt said. 'It's that sound one makes when one doesn't understand something and asks you to repeat it.'

It did sound like that. Sarbajeet steadied himself, and asked another question, 'Are you lonely?'

This time the response came after the question. It was an eerie answer. When played back, it sounded like two English words, this time in a female voice: *Get out.*

'Can you see us? How many of us are here?' Sarbajeet continued.

'*Bahut zyada!* (A lot!)' This was exactly what the reply sounded like.

Everyone stood in silence for a few moments, even as they tried to absorb what was really going on. The feeling of being watched by someone you cannot see had now started to sink in, and although it was a shared excitement, the fear had gripped every individual.

It was also getting darker and creepier. Some people began to shuffle their feet, not knowing whether to retreat or not. 'The horror of the moment was palpable,' Sarbajeet recalled. 'Most people there had never encountered ghosts before. There were sceptics in the lot, and now they heard these weird human sounds coming practically out of nowhere. You could just have knocked down some of those people with a feather. Meanwhile, we were contemplating whether we should go ahead.'

After a brief pause, a male voice resounded in the stillness of the stone corridor. The recorder picked up the sound. It was a chilling phrase uttered in Hindi: '*Jaao yahaan se*'.

'It's telling us to get out of here,' Sarbajeet translated for the benefit of the others.

'I heard it too,' said Bhatt. 'It's probably best if we left.'

It was a wise call on Bhatt's part. He knew from his own experience that spirits could be quite territorial, which could make them malevolent. In that particular location, as Pooja had explained earlier, there were spirits who didn't even know they had died. In such situations, possessiveness regarding territory is extreme. Bhatt was also responsible for the safety of all the media persons he had invited. As such, it was best if they obeyed the angry commands of the entities they could not see.

Sarbajeet nodded. As the group began to file out of the place, retracing their path, Sarbajeet said, 'We are leaving your territory as you asked us to. Don't worry, this is your house, and we won't trouble you any further. Best of luck to you.'

And then he said something important that is absolutely important to be said at the end of every paranormal investigation without fail, 'I request you to stay here and not follow any of us home. We shall not bother you anymore. Goodbye.'[2]

The experience was hair-raising, to say the least. The entire investigation was videotaped and is now available on the PAIRS channel on YouTube. The media persons covered the incident in their publications, and the mission was accomplished.

That night, none of the spirits went home with the people who had bravely ventured into the haunted fort, but what followed them home was a message—the world

---

[2]Here, Sarbajeet stressed on the importance of the spiritual goodbye, which is essential while closing any paranormal investigative session. Most spirits follow commands if they are given with the right tone and voice. It is crucial to issue an instruction for the entities to stay back, even if they did not make their presence felt in any way. Failing to do this might result in the invisible entity latching on to people and moving out with them to their abodes. More than anything, it also acts as a psychological closure, giving the humans a sense that the session has truly ended.

we live in and can see is certainly not the only world there is. Death is not the end of our existence, at least not always. The other side, in whatever shape or form, coexists with us, and perhaps it is our own limitations that prevent us from seeing or hearing it.

The successful expedition to the haunted fort was remarkable for many reasons, one of them being the evidence of sounds produced on recorded media. These voices, which were clearly human but whose origin was unexplained, lent credence to the fact that there was indeed someone out there, who could not be seen but was probably trying to make their presence felt.

In parapsychology, there is a specific term for such disembodied voices—electronic voice phenomena or EVP. For centuries, they have been closely studied not only by paranormal investigators, but also by reputable scientists and institutions. The vast body of research and experimentation of EVP has brought it much favour, making it the least criticized of all paranormal phenomena.

Electronic Voice Phenomenon

In parapsychology, EVP or electronic voice phenomenon is the occurrence of unexplained sounds on recorded electronic media, which are considered to be sounds produced by spirits.

EVP is one of the most commonly discussed topics in the paranormal world. The general theory is that these sounds are voices of spirits trying to communicate with us.

However, as they do not have the speech mechanism they had when they were alive, they do not have the ability to produce sounds that are within the human hearing range. However, the memory of producing sounds persists even after death. Because of this memory, the entities can produce sounds which might be in the lower-than-audible range of frequency (infrasonic sound) or higher-than-audible range of frequency (ultrasonic sound). If these infrasonic and ultrasonic sounds are captured and translated into our audible range, we may be able to hear and even comprehend what the spirits are trying to tell us.

Paranormal investigators highly value EVP recordings because they are considered the most authentic and irrefutable manifestation of the paranormal. As these sounds can be recorded and reproduced, they are more credible than visual evidence. An EVP recording is considered to be clear evidence of paranormal activity if it can be proven beyond doubt that it is not a hoax or a prank.

Historically, there has been evidence of EVP since the time of Alexander Graham Bell. When Bell developed his design for a listening device (which later became the prototype for the telephone), he was also working on a device that could enable him to access the afterlife. Specifically, he wished to communicate with his departed mother. He believed that communication with the afterlife was possible if we were on the same wavelength as them. He was never able to build such a device; however, several later devices did record unexplained voices, but not consistently or at will.

Another legendary scientist who lent credibility to electronic voice phenomena was Thomas Edison. In an interview that appeared in *Scientific Journal*, Edison suggested that it was possible to receive messages from spirits. However, such communication was very subtle and therefore required a highly sensitive recording device. Despite his beliefs, Edison himself never developed such a device.

Types of Electronic Voice Phenomena

The actual scope of electronic voice phenomena is quite vast, for the simple reason that there are many different types of sound recorders, both physical and app-based, and they operate on different principles. Overall, any device that can produce an EVP is called an in-trans communication device or ITC device. The most frequently used of these ITC devices is the common EVP recorder.

Apart from the differences arising from the recording device, parapsychology experts have categorized EVPs into four classes, depending on the quality of the recording.

Class A: These are the best EVP recordings, where the spoken words have a high degree of intelligibility. Most of the recordings Sarbajeet's team received at the Fort were Class A EVP recordings. Words and phrases such as '*Raus*' and '*Jaao yahaan se*' were heard by several people at the same time.

Class B: These are slightly vague EVP recordings. A human voice can be heard, but the words are not clear. One would need to guess what is being said. However, they still have a degree of credibility because it is a human-like voice.

Class C: These are the most ambiguous EVP recordings. They are not very clear human voices, but they might be other sounds such as hissing, blowing, scratching, coughing and such others. They are also of low quality and need to be amplified with higher sensitivity devices to understand the sounds.

Class R: This is a unique and very rare type of EVP recording. The human voice is clear, but the words are reversed. The reversal applies to the individual syllables of the word. At first glance, they therefore sound like gibberish. However, if played in reverse, intelligible words can be obtained. The reason why some EVP recordings are reversed is not known, but it might be that the spirits producing them can cause a higher degree of intelligent haunting.

Paranormal investigators consider Class A, B and C recordings, but they don't give much consideration to Class R recordings. They are generally kept aside and only taken into account when there is no other evidence of haunting.

Criticism of Electronic Voice Phenomena

It is understandable that EVP attracts its fair share of criticism from its detractors. This comes mostly from those who are sceptical about the paranormal world in general, and do not believe that there is an 'other world' populated by spirits. However, it is worth noting that EVPs cannot be denied. While many of them are outright rejected as hoaxes, the fact remains that genuine EVPs do exist and are heard, but critics offer other explanations for these sounds.

The most scientific criticism of EVP is that it is an example of pareidolia. To an extent, we all suffer from pareidolia. Pareidolia is the tendency of the human brain to find familiar patterns in things we see. Visual pareidolia is quite common. The best example of this is seeing shapes in clouds. Here, the shapes do not really exist, but our brain conditions us into thinking that they do. Similarly, EVP might be a case of auditory pareidolia. These could be random sounds captured from the surroundings, which our brain conditions us into recognizing as human voices articulating certain words. This theory is somewhat strengthened by the fact that each person tends to interpret EVP sounds in the language they know—a Frenchman will hear these words in French, a Mexican in Spanish.

The possibility of physics doing its thing cannot be ignored either. The sounds might be produced due to interference from waves or cross-modulations with a neighbouring medium. It is also possible that these are amplified voices of a person within the range that have been carried along with the sound waves.

During our discussions on this subject, Sarbajeet and Pooja shared with me many experiences with EVP recordings. In fact, their reputation as paranormal investigators was bolstered by the fact that they obtained such recordings in several places where they conducted investigations, often in the presence of large groups of people.

We spoke about their experiences at Holkar Bridge in

Pune. This haunted location was known to be an abode of many restless spirits. During one investigation here, the PAIRS team clearly captured many EVP sounds. The most distinct of those was of a spirit who identified himself as Srinivas. Srinivas claimed he was a slave living in that region in 1120 AD. Upon further inquiry, Sarbajeet realized that Srinivas's death had been sudden, which was why his spirit still believed he was alive. Using these details, Sarbajeet could release the spirit from the location where he was trapped for centuries.[3]

The Bengaluru Ghost Hunt

Another paranormal hunt was conducted by PAIRS in Bengaluru. This was in association with another organization, the Indian Paranormal Society. This joint investigation was conducted in a haunted forest in Bengaluru that ran along the state highway.

Preliminary research showed that the place had a terrible history. Located within the city but away from the hustle and bustle, the forested area was abused by locals and passers-by for various nefarious activities. Criminals hid the spoils of their crimes here, including the bodies of the people they had murdered. Druggies and perverts used this spot as a hideout for many years until severe police crackdowns put an end to it.

Today, after much effort by the law-and-order authorities, this area is no longer a haven for criminals. However, the sighs of the dead still persist, and can be

[3]This case is discussed in detail in Chapter 3.

occasionally heard if one is quiet and attentive. People passing by this area, and even motorists driving on the adjoining highway, have claimed to see abnormal apparitions on the edge of the forest. They have been approached for lifts. If one stops here for any reason, for instance to answer nature's call, or if their car breaks down, they might hear inhuman wails and screams coming from inside the forest.

To ascertain the veracity of these hair-raising reports, Sarbajeet, Pooja, and a member of the Indian Paranormal Society went into the forest armed with paranormal research equipment. They were met with responses on their devices at the fringe of the forest. This led them inward into the wilderness, till they came to a different coloured mud patch on the ground, the size of a human.

The team spent several minutes analysing the mud patch through observation. Fear mounted in them as they realized they were absolutely cut off from civilization. Then, at a particular spot on the mud patch, their devices went berserk. It was a sight to see the lights flickering on all devices in the absolute darkness.

Getting a grip on their fear, they decided to explore this spot further. But they could not make much headway as they could not disturb the area by digging up the ground.

As they walked further inside, Sarbajeet received a very clear audio input on the PAIRS Spirit Box app. It was a single word in a human voice that made the entire team stop right there and listen to it again and again in disbelief. That word was '*Sara*'.

They asked a string of questions in a bid to know more about who Sara was. Sarbajeet used a K2 meter to ask

Sara questions—whether she was a native, when she had died, whether her death was natural or an act of crime, and so on. However, after a few initial responses, Sara's spirit stopped answering and disappeared somewhere in the middle of the forest. And she was lost forever.

Although the investigation was cut short at that point, many replies were clearly heard. It was recorded by the team and is now available on their YouTube channel for the world to hear.

In conclusion, EVP voices are the kind of evidence that all paranormal researchers yearn to obtain. Curiously, some investigators seem to get a lot of such responses, while others don't make much headway. 'It might be due to the approach of the investigating team,' says Sarbajeet. 'Spirits do not respond when spoken to harshly or rudely, or if something about the investigator ticks them off. It is important that the investigators make sure that the entities feel safe and are not threatened in any way. In most cases, the spirits are more afraid of us than we are of them.'

When a paranormal investigator does get an EVP response, it can be channelled in the right way to open a line of communication with the spirit. A conversation can be initiated by asking yes-or-no questions, or objective questions that require one-word replies. This can enable the investigating team to learn a lot more about the entity and the location they are investigating.

Evidence of confirmed and genuine EVP proves one thing beyond a shadow of doubt—there is an afterlife. There are entities out there who can see us but whom we cannot see. Whether they are our dead or not is debatable. But there is definitely intelligent life in the air around us. The frequent occurrence of such EVP also shows that this other world wants to communicate with us. We are probably still hindered by the absence of the right technology to get them to talk to us, but imagine the new world that might open up to us once we have such technology.

PLAYBACKS OF THE PAST

Residual Haunting

'The world is its own enduring monument.'

—Joseph Rodes Buchanan

In the suburbs of Navi Mumbai, a strange case was brought to the PAIRS office. Sarbajeet and Pooja listened with rapt attention as Ramdas Tiwari's case was narrated to them. Tiwari was a landowner who had inherited a piece of land from his father a few years ago. The land had lain fallow for many decades. Although it was a sizeable piece of land, he had not been able to use it in any manner whatsoever.

The farm was in disuse because it was believed to be haunted by the spirits of a young couple. On certain full moon nights, people saw these spirits sitting on the platform of one of the two wells in the field. The couple would appear to be very much in love and fully immersed in each other. After a few minutes, they would get up, and walk hand in hand to the other end of the field, where there was a larger well. They would hover in the air above this well and then suddenly dive into it. People who witnessed this hair-raising moment claimed that it was so real that they could even hear a loud splash as the lovers plunged into the well.

However, nothing was ever found. When multiple witnesses reported the same occurrence, the farm earned the reputation of being haunted. Their farm hands stopped reporting to duty, and no one wanted to go near the wells. The field soon turned barren as it fell into disuse.

Tiwari had tried to re-irrigate his fields a year ago. With much difficulty, he had found and hired farm labourers from another village. However, no sooner had they tried to irrigate the farm than the hauntings resumed. But this time, something even more dramatic happened. One morning, a young farmer went missing. His body was found floating in the same well. The villagers quickly surmised that the man had been killed by the spirits of the well. The field fell into a state of complete desolation after this.

Now Tiwari wanted to get to the root of the matter. As a rich man, it did not hurt him much if one of his many properties lay unused, but he could not get the mystery of the haunting out of his head. So a date and time was set for the investigators to go to the field and try to get to the bottom of the haunting. They were to do this on the next full moon night. They would visit with their clutch of ghost-hunting equipment and spend the night in the field.

Sarbajeet and Pooja brought with them their EMF meters, an electronic device for recording voice phenomena, a night vision camera, an infrared thermometer, and a set of walkie-talkies, among other devices. When they arrived on the farm at 9:00 p.m., they found it warmly bathed in the silvery semi-darkness of a moonlit night. But the ground was dry and cracked; it was evident that nothing had been sown there for years.

They spent the whole night in the field, periodically pacing between the two wells which were about 200 metres apart, but did not find anything remarkable. The only thing they noted was that everything was eerily quiet. Even dogs avoided the farm, although they could clearly be heard barking in the adjoining farms. Finding nothing of note until morning, they packed up and left.

Sarbajeet and Pooja returned the next full moon night and still found nothing. They positioned their devices in strategic positions, but nothing untoward happened. At this point, they would have given up and reported to Tiwari that there was nothing unnatural about his farm, but they stopped short of it. Pooja's psychic powers told her to persist.

Something was just biding its time, she felt. And she was right.

In the middle of the night, around 2:30 a.m., a bizarre incident took place near the larger well. As Pooja bent over to look, she was nearly thrown off her feet by a cloud of gloom that suddenly rose like a mushroom from the well. It was a strong feeling of negativity, the likes of which she had never experienced before. Recounting the incident, she says, 'A gut-wrenching dark energy gripped me thrice on that second full moon night. Though I did not see anything, I knew that there was something to be explored.'

This cloud of gloom brought her back to the farm

on the third full moon night, and on this occasion, their persistence was rewarded.

At 11:30 p.m., Sarbajeet spotted a glow on the platform around the first well that was closest to them. It was a white light, like a shining orb, and it was hovering in the air about two or three feet above the ground. He directed Pooja to watch it, but she could not see the glow. Sarbajeet then began to walk over to the spot. As he did so, he could see the glow more clearly, it was a nebulous, distended structure, but even in its highly abstract form, it bore the vestiges of a human form.

As silently as he could, he took out his EMF meter. He went to the well, close to where the glow still was, and kept watch on the meter. Typically, any paranormal presence creates an aberration in the surrounding electromagnetic field. Sarbajeet waited to see a sign of some kind on the meter, but there was nothing. He then steeled himself and kept the meter right on the well's platform. He expected the lights to turn on in full force, but nothing happened.

When he stood up, he could make out two shapes, which looked very much humanlike.

This was surprising to me, and I had to stop Sarbajeet's narration at this point and ask him if he really saw two figures.

To that, Sarbajeet said, 'Let me tell you how horrific this scene was. There we were, in the middle of this vast empty farm at night, not a living person in sight, and all of a sudden there are these two white, cloud-like, disembodied figures by the well. To the ordinary human eye, they would not mean anything. Maybe they would just evoke fear because of their vague form, but I could make out that they were the shapes of a man and a woman. I supposed that they were the lovers the villagers were talking about.'

'Did you not try to take pictures of it on your phone?' I asked, and immediately knew it was a rookie question.

Sarbajeet answered promptly, 'We do that every time we come across any such activity, but these pictures never materialize. The wavelength at which the spiritual world operates is not discernible to the human senses.'

In fact, none of the devices recorded anything on this occasion. Without evidence, this meant nothing.

Sarbajeet stepped back and attempted to see the scene through the lens of his night vision camera. When he did, the spot appeared normal; there was no discernible light.

He told Pooja what he was seeing, and Pooja decided to go and stand near the larger well—the same spot where she had encountered the cloud of gloom. According to the legend, the spirits that Sarbajeet had seen would walk to this larger well and take a plunge. If there was any activity there, Pooja would sense it. So Sarbajeet remained at the first well while Pooja stationed herself at the second. They kept contact via their walkie-talkies.

About half an hour later, Sarbajeet saw the globes of light once again; they were moving. They were now hovering higher in the air, as if the spirits had stood up, and they vaguely looked like two people walking. What appeared to be their faces were turned towards each other, and they seemed oblivious to everything else. Even when Sarbajeet dared to approach them, and eventually gathered the courage to pass his hand through the glow, it went right through it without any resistance. 'I knew at that point that they weren't harmless. They were probably apparitions trying to fulfil some incomplete destiny,' said Sarbajeet.

He whispered to Pooja over his walkie-talkie that she should prepare herself. He followed the disembodied spectres hovering in the air several feet above the ground. Their movements were slow; it was the gait of two lovers who did not want to part.

When they were about to reach the other well, Pooja was ready. She still could not see anything, but she could see Sarbajeet moving towards her at a slow, skulking pace, his eyes fixed on a spot in the air above him. She realized what he could see and moved away to clear the path to the well. She was about ten paces away from the well when she experienced that feeling of great despair again. She looked up sharply, and that was when she also saw the glow. 'I saw it then. It was hanging right up there, a sphere of light moving very slowly towards the well,' says Pooja.

As the light approached her, Pooja was bathed in the cloud of gloom that she had encountered before. This time it affected her so badly that she had to hold her head and sit down by the edge of the well.

Sarbajeet came running towards her as the lovers reached the brink of the well. Pooja was wildly emotional, with tears flowing out of her eyes. That was the point when Sarbajeet saw the spirits hovering above the edge of the well. The impact of that moment was so profound that, despite being an experienced paranormal investigator, Sarbajeet forgot that what he was seeing was not alive anymore, and lunged to grab the couple before they dived in.

All his hands touched was empty air as a loud splash was heard.

Pooja stood up immediately and ran to look inside the well. Waving her hands wildly, she tried to save whatever it was that had attempted to end its own life.

❧

It took the investigators several weeks to arrive at some kind of conclusion about the bizarre events they had witnessed on the farm. Never before had their devices failed to record something that they both perceived so clearly. To add to that, there were reports from several previous witnesses, as well as a death, which lent weight to assertions about the haunting. It was similar to what the witnesses had described, though their descriptions were peppered with exaggerated details. Sarbajeet conducted an extensive amount of research to arrive at a conclusion. Soon enough, he discovered what was causing it.

He found that what they had experienced on the farm was a phenomenon known as residual haunting. Just as they had experienced it, residual haunting leaves absolutely no trace. Apart from the instantaneous visual and auditory manipulation it causes, such as hallucinations, there is nothing to attest to its reality. To understand it better, let's study what this means.

Residual Haunting

Residual haunting is a specific kind of haunting wherein the immediate surroundings and certain materials in the vicinity project visual and auditory 'reproductions' of an event that might have occurred in the past, often playing it back regularly in the same way as it had occurred.

It is a lot like video playback. In this case, the video is played without a screen, mid-air, like a holographic image. There are several reported instances of residual hauntings around the world, where often only the visuals are observed over and over again, but in some rare cases these visuals are also accompanied by sounds.

The causes of these phenomena have been studied by several noted scientists and other experts from around the world. One of the progenitors of this concept was Charles Babbage (considered to be the inventor of the computer), who stated that every sound that is produced leaves a lingering impact on its surroundings for a period of time. Babbage speculated that this impact stays on for some time before it fades out completely. Today, we know this to be true. Sound is propagated in the form of longitudinal waves, which is nothing but the vibration of particles of the medium through which it passes (in most cases, air). Even when the sound has effectively passed through, the particles keep vibrating for a short period of time. This is also what causes the persistence of sound on our eardrums for about a tenth of a second after the source has stopped emitting the sound. The same applies to vision; the retina holds any image for a tenth of a second, even after the source of the stimulus has been removed.

The concept of residual haunting is an extension of this, involving some speculation. There is a belief that even the surroundings and certain materials can store these energies, giving rise to something known as *object memory*. Object memory projects these energies into the surroundings, effectively causing the same incident to appear, just as in playback.

Another noteworthy piece of research in the field of residual haunting comes from the Welsh philosopher and proponent of the afterlife theory H.H. Price, who was also the president of the Society of Psychical Research (1939–40 and 1960–61). Price suggested that there is a medium known as ether pervading our environment, which connects the physical and spiritual worlds. When a person leaves the physical world and has to pass on to the spiritual world, they have to pass through this ether. The ether thus retains the traces of memories. Though the presence of such ether, as Price suggested, has not yet been discovered, it could explain the phenomenon of residual haunting.

Sarbajeet suggests that some materials may be able to capture audio and visual memories better than others. These include building materials such as iron, stone and slate, materials which were used in medieval architecture. Their ability to capture memories increases when they are oxidized or rusted. Paranormal research experts believe that these materials can record images and sounds just like a tape recorder, and then play them back on certain occasions, usually at regular intervals.

However, there are many criticisms of this theory. The biggest objection is that the recording and playback of the images and sounds is not scientifically possible without a specific device. For example, audio cassettes and VHS tapes could play back recorded sounds and images due to a magnetic head equipped in them. A mere spool of tape is not enough to record or playback. Just as one cannot see or hear anything by merely coming near a tape (without a magnetic head to play it back), these materials alone should not be able to record or play sounds and images. As a result of this criticism, all proposed theories of residual haunting have been relegated to the status of pseudoscience.

This leaves things open-ended, and without a proper explanation. The fact is that there are many recorded instances of residual haunting around the world, and in fact, this is one of the most common type of hauntings. Notable examples are: the ghost of Anne Boleyn in the Tower of London, the Brown Lady of Raynham Hall, the ghost sightings at the Stanley Hotel in Colorado (which inspired Stephen King's novel *The Shining*), the sightings of colonial prisoners at Edinburgh Castle in Scotland, the Oriental Theatre in Chicago (where 600 people perished in a fire in 1903, and their ghosts are sometimes still spotted), and so on. There are also theories that some UFOs that leave no trace behind could be nothing more than residual hauntings projected into the sky.

As long as these hauntings are observed, there can be no end to this debate. While critics are ready to denounce all proposed theories to explain residual hauntings as false science, the fact that more and more people are coming out and reporting such sightings is also irrefutable. Until then, it will remain a mystery as to what causes the playback of these painful memories—is it the conditions of the surroundings, the right materials or architecture, conducive weather conditions, or just the deep emotional energies of the deceased?

Sarbajeet applied these studies to their experience between the two wells at the farm. They could draw a clear analogy between the two. While digging into the history of the place, Sarbajeet discovered that a tragedy had indeed occurred at the spot about 70 years ago. A young couple, who were not permitted to marry because of caste differences, decided to end their lives there. The last night they spent at the well was certainly emotionally intense, so intense that their emotions seeped into the surroundings and lingered for decades. When they took the final plunge, the situation was so gut-wrenchingly horrid that it even left behind an audio imprint in the form of a splash. It was evidence of the depth of the couple's feelings on their last night that the scene persisted at the site for several decades following the incident.

But now it was fading, for Sarbajeet had seen only a glow instead of complete figures, and Pooja had not seen them at all. They reported this to Tiwari, the landlord. He was saddened to know that the tragedy had occurred on his farm, but also relieved that it was fading away. Regarding the death of the young farmer, it was determined to be an accident. Perhaps he was so overwrought on witnessing the scene that he had lurched ahead and fallen into the well. 'That seems to be the most plausible explanation,' says Sarbajeet. 'When I saw them diving into the well, even I felt that it was too real, and lunged ahead. It is possible that it would have seemed much more real to the unfortunate farmer. He might have leapt in to save the couple.'

As Sarbajeet and Pooja had surmised, the haunting receded over the next few months, and then stopped completely. As word of their report spread through the village, the farm hands gradually reported back to work, and the field was irrigated once again.

The best-known example of residual haunting in India is the Shaniwar Wada Fort in Pune. Steeped in a rich Maratha Peshwa history, this stunning fort is completely deserted by sundown, despite a large number of locals and tourists visiting it in the daytime. If one explores the fort, it comes across as being infested with a number of paranormal phenomena, of which its resident ghost has gained the highest degree of notoriety.

The history of the Shaniwar Wada Fort dates back to 1730, when it was built as a residence for the valiant Peshwa Bajirao I. Built with the most expensive variety of teak and stone, the fort was an awe-inspiring structure housing all royalty or aristocrats of the time. However, for all its stately grandeur, the fort was beset with negativity right from its earliest days. It is said that a woman whose husband was sentenced by the Peshwa for his offences laid a curse on the fort. And from then on, it was plagued by a series of catastrophes.

It began with the wedge between Peshwa Bajirao I and his wife Kashibai, driven by the former's love affair with another woman named Mastani. While Kashibai pined away for her husband, Bajirao and Mastani's love was never requited, and both of them had sorrowful deaths. The tragedies continued into the subsequent generations. Bajirao's eldest son Nanasaheb had three sons. The oldest of them was Vishwasrao, who was brutally killed in the

First Battle of Panipat. The second son Madhavrao went into depression on account of his elder brother's passing, and himself met with an untimely death. But the most horrific death was that of the youngest son Narayanrao, who became a peshwa at the age of 16.

As Narayanrao was a minor, his uncle Raghunathrao was appointed regent. However, Raghunathrao and his wife Anandibai did not like this arrangement as they felt that the former should have been appointed peshwa. As the animosity between them grew, Raghunathrao sought the assistance of the extremely ruthless Gardi tribe to kill his nephew. The evil deed was carried out on one unholy full moon night. The Gardi assassins stormed into the Shaniwar Wada Fort and killed everyone that stood in their way. Narayanrao was asleep upstairs, unaware that the fort had been broken into. When the assassins broke into his room, he woke up and ran out of the room in sheer terror and up the long corridor to his uncle's room. He screamed for his uncle to help him. In Marathi, he said, '*Kaka, mala vachva! Mala vachva!* (Uncle, save me! Save me!)'

But imagine his horror when his uncle stepped out of his room and stood still as a rock, even when he saw the assassins chasing his nephew with swords. The assassins threw themselves over the stunned peshwa and stabbed him all over his body. He cried and screamed until his last breath, shocked at his uncle's treachery even as his body was torn into pieces. When the act of unspeakable cruelty was over, Raghunathrao ordered the tribesmen to take away his nephew's mortal remains and dump them into the nearby Mutha River.

The locals say that this tragedy plays out in the fort even today. No one dares enter the fort or even lurk near it. But on certain full moon nights, the lights of the Shaniwar Wada Fort can be seen even from a distance. They light up by themselves on a certain upper floor, and the surroundings are rent by the young peshwa's pitiful cries: '*Kaka, mala vachva! Mala vachva!*'

This is a clear example of residual haunting. The tragedy was of such humongous proportions that it was recorded for posterity in the sturdy teak and stone that the fort was made of. The incident left its imprint on the fort.

People are not allowed to enter the fort after sunset, but a few intrepid adventurers set up camp near the fort on full moon nights and keep watch. Many have returned with the mind-numbing experience of hearing the cries of the young peshwa in the middle of the night. This phenomenon defies all logical explanation but fits very well with the known concepts of a residual haunting.

~

To summarize, there is no real solution to residual haunting. There is nothing a human being can do to stop it. However, like everything else, emotions and energies dissipate over time. The imprints left by such catastrophic incidents in history slowly fade away and eventually disappear completely.

They are different from ghosts because there are no entities involved; it's like watching a really old film on loop. Therefore, the residual haunting does no direct harm apart from the fear it invokes, which can lead certain people to behave in dangerous ways with respect to themselves or others. However, it is important to note that residual ghosts are harmless. They are just projections and have no material presence. They cannot react to their surroundings. If you ever come across such a haunting, you can safely watch it unfold. You do not have to be afraid, because fear is the real danger. Knowing what residual hauntings are, and being prepared when visiting places with a rich history, can be a lifesaver for those who venture into such territories.

TRAPPED IN THE LIVING WORLD

Intelligent Haunting

'We are all of us haunted and haunting.'

—Chuck Palahniuk

The infamous Holkar Bridge in Pune has a bad reputation—that of being haunted. In the daytime, one would not think much of the bridge as it looks like any other normal bridge with the usual flow of vehicular and pedestrian traffic. But when night falls, human activity dwindles because of an inexplicable fear. Rumours of serious paranormal activity hound this place, and the presence of an ancient graveyard just across the bridge doesn't help. People talk in hushed voices about bodies found in the stream under the bridge, often with terrified expressions frozen on their dead faces, and at times mutilated in unimaginably gruesome ways. While there are the usual sceptics, there are also a significant number of people who have witnessed unexplained phenomena such as apparitions and disembodied voices.

This terrifying reputation has arisen from many historical stories. The Holkar Bridge was built in the early

1800s by Yashwantrao Holkar, after whom it was named. Yashwantrao Holkar was the Maharaja of Indore, who rebelled against the policies of Peshwa Bajirao II. This led to the Battle of Pune, during which Holkar's troops camped in what is now the park below Holkar Bridge. Later, the same spot was used as a military camp by the British. Over the years, the tragedies of wars and their aftermath gave rise to the many hair-raising stories about the place.

Sarbajeet and Pooja narrated to me the details of their investigation at Holkar Bridge in December 2019. They had gone there in the dead of the night after conducting intensive research on the history of the bridge and listening to the stories told by locals. Some people had claimed to have seen a mass of white smoke floating through the park area, sometimes brushing against them and causing goosebumps. A few willing locals had also spoken of the bodies occasionally found floating in the stream near the bridge. These deaths often went unreported and uninvestigated, and most of the bodies were not even identified.

As their curiosity was undeniably piqued, Sarbajeet, Pooja and two other team-members of PAIRS reached the Holkar Bridge on the cold night. Vehicular movement on the bridge was minimal. After thoroughly scanning the bridge and the graveyard, they came to the shallow stream under the bridge. The stream was hardly a stream at all, just an oversized puddle of dirty water. Across the stream, they saw a spacious park that was the exact spot where the military encampments used to be. After a preliminary investigation, they took out their equipment to do a more detailed study. That was when horrific things started happening.

The night suddenly took a turn for the worse when they came down the bridge to the stream. As they walked on, one of the team-members suddenly felt something brushing against her arm. Thinking that it might be a hallucination caused by anticipative fear, she didn't mention it to anyone. But moments later, the man walking ahead of her also felt something, and he immediately retracted his arm. This was when the group realized that there was something afoot.

Pooja had already equipped herself with a ghost meter. The device had been detecting some kind of activity for a while, but it intensified dramatically when they came to the spot under the bridge. The device started blinking continuously. In the darkness of the night, the constant blinking of the lights on the ghost meter seemed even more eerie. She then took a deep breath, and said out loud, 'Hello. I am Pooja. I am here with my friends. We just want to communicate with you. I have a device in my hand that can tell us about your presence. All you have to do is to come close to it.'

Sarbajeet added, 'We are not here to harm you, and we know that you can feel our presence. You also know that we are only here to understand you better. Let us know if you are around.'

There was a moment of silence, and during the calm, Pooja felt that the meter in her hand blinked. She immediately brought it to Sarbajeet's attention. The team now needed a confirmation. A second request was made by Sarbajeet, 'Thank you for indicating your presence.

For confirmation, could you please make our device flash again?'

This time the blinking was prolonged. They had entered what paranormal investigators call 'communication mode'.

Sarbajeet described his elation to me in the following words, 'It is extremely rare that the ghost meter lights up fully like that. It means that we are in the proximity of a strong paranormal presence. Of course, it's scary to the core, but for us it is also very much exciting.'

The ghost meter was still lit up. As Pooja was continuing her investigation, something very odd happened. The team member who had felt something brushing against her arm earlier exclaimed that the battery of her camera had drained by more than 40 per cent. It was just unexplainable how the battery had gone down so suddenly.

For confirmation, Pooja asked, 'Are you draining the energy from our battery?'

Almost immediately, the reply came—it was a strong blinking on the ghost meter. Simultaneously, their backup battery also drained.

Sarbajeet explains, 'Spirits, when they need to manifest themselves in any way, need energy. They try to derive this energy from electrical devices and appliances in their vicinity. This is the reason why lights flicker, or machines behave erratically when there is a paranormal presence. The draining of the battery meant that the spirit was particularly communicative.'

Now realizing that the spirit was willing to communicate, the team decided to try out a special device to have a direct conversation with the entity. This was the PSB7[4], which converts bursts of inaudible sound energy into audible signals that are understandable to the human ear. It was perfect for attempting paranormal communication.

This time, Sarbajeet took on the mantle of communication, and an extremely bizarre episode followed. By now, night had fallen. There was hardly a vehicle to be seen on the bridge above. Apart from the stray nocturnal sounds of animals and insects, there was absolute silence everywhere. In this silence, Sarbajeet spoke loud and clear, 'Hello. I am Sarbajeet. I am here to talk to you. Would you like to talk?'

For a while, the spirit box made only weird knocking sounds. Then, amidst all the noise, one clear word was heard—*'Srinivas'*.

Once again, the excitement of the team peaked. Not only did they have a communicative spirit (which is considered one of the highest points in a paranormal investigation), but they had a spirit who was potentially giving accurate information.

Sarbajeet indicated Pooja to record the rest of the investigation on her phone as well, as the camera batteries had trained. However, they were in for a shock as even the phone batteries were draining significantly. Pooja's battery went down from 90% to 16% in a matter of seconds. It was surmised that the spirit was very close, so close that it could feed on the energies from the devices. They decided to wrap this up quickly and get

---

[4]PSB stands for Portable Spirit Box, a common device used by paranormal investigators.

as much as possible of it on record.

'Is that your name, Mr Srinivas? Please talk to us,' Sarbajeet urged. 'This device here will help us understand you.'

Sarbajeet held the spirit box in front of him, trying to keep his arm as steady as he could. This time there was some radio noise box.

Encouraged by this, Sarbajeet went on. 'Yes, we heard that. But we did not understand it. Please, can you repeat it?'

This was followed by a series of gurgling noises on the app, which did not make sense. For a while, it appeared that the spirit was trying to communicate in a South Indian language, perhaps Tamil, but no clear words could be made out.

One thing, however, was established—that the spirit was communicative. The team now had to find the right medium to enable it to continue its conversation. This was when Sarbajeet decided to use an app that was well-suited for this purpose. To put it simply, the app has a built-in bank of words, which spirits can use to communicate with humans.

Now, no sooner did Sarbajeet attempt to use the app than two words came up quite clearly: *'Eleventh century.'*

It was beyond any question now—the team was communicating with a spirit of a human named Srinivas, who hailed from the eleventh century. More questions followed, and more startling revelations were made. Words such as 'cupboard', 'tape', and finally 'slave', shed more light on the nature of the circumstances.

The inference made by the team was that Srinivas

has been a slave during that time and had perhaps died a gruesome death (the 'cupboard' might have referred to one of the torture devices that were in common use at that time). The impact of his death was so deep on his soul that he had not been able to move on. By a series of stepwise questioning and subsequent replies on the app, these inferences were more or less confirmed.

When the facts were all out, the team sat in dead silence. They had the feeling as if someone was listening to them. Listening very closely.

Sarbajeet saw that his battery had almost died out, and the app would turn off any second. The spirit box was the only thing that was still functioning. It was time to close the investigation.

Keeping his voice steady, Sarbajeet said, 'Srinivas, we understand that your life must have been difficult. But we are in the 21st century now. Everything has changed. The world is different. You cannot stay here anymore. You can now go in peace to the other world that awaits you.'

An eerie silence followed Sarbajeet's little closing speech. The team waited for several minutes. The mobile phone shut down completely. About five minutes later, the park lights flickered in the distance. Under the blinking lights, they could discern a shadow walking by quickly.

Srinivas had apparently left for good. At least that is what the team wanted to believe. Without the means to investigate further, they decided to call it a day.[5]

---

[5]The entire investigation has been uploaded on the YouTube channel of PAIRS, named Ghost Encounters.

Intelligent Haunting

The episode described above is what paranormal experts call an intelligent haunting. This is a specific type of haunting in which the spiritual presence is able to communicate with the physical world in certain ways. In the aforementioned scenario, the responses on the devices, the spirit's ability to understand which device to respond on, the consumption of energy, the flickering of the lights, and the tactile sensations produced (such as goosebumps, sweating, cold chills, suffocation, the feeling of being grazed)—are all indications that the spirit was able to physically manifest in some ways.

Horror movies and literature largely play on this ability of spirits, often in an exaggerated form. In these narratives, spirits are shown to perform powerful physical tasks that would require a lot of strength and energy even from a human. Sarbajeet's take on this is, 'Spirits are rarely capable of performing any major physical tasks. The actions that they can perform, if at all, are simple, subtle and often imperceptible—things that wouldn't make horror movies or literature so interesting and fun to watch if they were faithfully depicted.'

Before we proceed, let us establish a definition of intelligent haunting:

Intelligent haunting is a high-level physical manifestation of a spiritual entity, which shows itself in certain ways that the human senses can perceive and understand. It is an intelligent consciousness, which can understand other consciousness around it and communicate with them.

Intelligent haunting is markedly different from

residual haunting, the other common form of haunting. Residual haunting is merely the playback of visual and auditory memories from a moment in the past, whereas intelligent haunting is a kind of live haunting, where the spiritual presence can interact with its surroundings. While residual haunting is considered absolutely safe because it is just an image, intelligent haunting can be dangerous if the spirit still harbours strong emotions. There is also a kind of periodicity and localization of residual hauntings. They occur at specific times and in particular locations, which are a reproduction of where they had first occurred. Intelligent hauntings are not focused like these, although the spirit may still be confined to a particular geographical location.

Paranormal experts advise amateurs to take precautions when dealing with an intelligent haunting presence. There is no pattern in which they might act. A misstep could also turn fatal for a variety of reasons, including the absolute shock it can cause to the onlooker. 'The most dangerous scenario is when the spirit is vengeful and the human is unable to connect with the spirit. Spirits with strong emotional baggage from the time they lived can do severely harmful things,' says Sarbajeet.

It is important to understand at the outset if the haunting is residual or intelligent. It is an intelligent haunting if the being is able to manifest in any specific way, such as sending signals on electronic devices, causing tactile sensations, or even merely generating a strong negative vibe in the area. Residual hauntings are just reproduced images and they generally don't produce a negative vibe, but it depends on how the viewer perceives it. Residual hauntings occur in fixed patterns, such as periodic patterns (like every full moon night, or a particular date), or thematic patterns (like always making a particular faucet drip water). There is no variation in the way they occur. However, intelligent hauntings can be unpredictable as their nature can change at every occurrence.

Precautions in Ghost-Hunting

Based on his experiences, Sarbajeet outlines a set of instructions to be followed when dealing with a supernatural entity. These are culled from the investigations and observations of the members of his paranormal team.

1. Be respectful towards the entity. As soon as you reach a location, introduce yourself by announcing your name out loud, and speak politely and clearly in case there is any disturbance in the surrounding atmosphere, such as noise caused by external factors.
2. State clearly that your only purpose is to talk and communicate. Ask the entity's permission to have a conversation.
3. Try to communicate in different languages, especially the prevailing local ones.
4. Conduct thorough research on the history of the place beforehand.
5. Do not rely too much on your electronic devices. They are just indicators; you are the real instrument.
6. Make sure you carry flashlights, a first-aid kit, an adequate amount of water (paranormal encounters can be dehydrating), and a regular backup phone that

will stay switched off. This phone is your backup for normal communication in case the batteries of your other phones die out.

7. Wear long pants and boots. This is to protect you from snake bites, scorpion stings, and other such dangers.
8. Stay safe and back off at any sign of aggression. Retreat after saying a polite goodbye.
9. Do not let fear rule your emotions. Most spirits aren't vindictive. Almost all haunting-related deaths have occurred because the subject succumbed to fear.

Along with these pointers, Sarbajeet adds, 'Inexperienced amateurs are advised not to go ghost-hunting on their own. It must be noted that these trips are fraught with danger. It's not just about ghosts and spirits. In fact, they are the least harmful of the things you might encounter. At the most, they might cause you extreme fear and you might fall unconscious. The bigger danger comes from wild animals, snakes, scorpions and the like. Once you step into savage territory, things get unpredictable. Desolate locations are the abodes of animals, and they can get highly territorial. Then there is the threat from people. Locals might not like you prowling about in their territory, even if you have permission from the authorities. On one or two occasions, we nearly ran into such trouble. Some locations can also be the haunts of perverts and people with criminal tendencies who might resort to any measure to keep their activities secret.'

The PAIRS team witnessed another instance of intelligent haunting at an abandoned university building in Khandala. Constructed in 1832 during the colonial period, this university building boasts of a rich history. There was a time when either the building itself or the space where it now stands was used as a kind of prison for criminal offenders. Criminals from Britain, Germany and France were housed in the cells. Some of the rooms still have strange wire-like structures, whose purpose is unknown. Even now, centuries later, the place bears a deserted look. And even a strong-hearted person would feel uneasy if they had to walk down its halls in the dead of the night.

Sarbajeet and his team encountered a string of hauntings while investigating the building and its premises. Their devices recorded the early indications, behaving in a highly erratic manner as soon as they entered the vicinity of the structure. These signals then turned to more concrete evidence such as sounds of someone running, screams from the inner rooms and the creaking of furniture for no apparent reason.

With her psychic abilities, Pooja was able to sense a strong negative vibe in the rooms with the wires. She claims that these wires were torture devices. Many a prisoner was strung to death with the wires, and their disgruntled ghosts still roam in the premises of the sprawling building, perhaps looking for a way to eternal liberation.

Sarbajeet signs off by saying, 'Ghosts are not all bad. That is a misconception. Even those who can interact with humans are usually in a deep emotional well of their own and if gently prodded, they will tell their sordid tale by whatever mechanism they have at their disposal. It's a paranormal investigator's duty to be able to sense the sentiment of the spirit, and be prepared to back off at the right time. Falling prey to curiosity and proceeding recklessly is often the path to grave danger.'

GHOSTS OF THE DEAR DEPARTED

Interactive Ghosts and Spirits

'I don't believe in ghosts or paranormal activity, but one time I think I saw—I might have seen—no, I think I did see a ghost.'

—Jason Blum

On 20 June 2013, Pooja's father died of cancer at the age of 67. Pooja had always been strongly connected to her father. He was deeply involved in spiritualism and was her guru in spiritual matters. As an only child, Pooja benefitted from her father's knowledge and expertise. His demise at a relatively young age shattered her.

However, life had to go on. Pooja focused on her life with her mother and her two sons. She considered this to be a new lease of life and moved on. She knew there was no other way but to keep her father's memories close to her and accept the challenges of life as they came.

However, little did she know how literally true this was going to be. Several experiences in coming years made her realize that her departed father was closer to her than she thought.

In 2017, Pooja's mother was due for a heart surgery. Though it was a minor procedure, the fact that it was a cardiac surgery kept the entire family on tenterhooks. Tensions ran high, which is understandable when an elderly member of the family must go under the surgeon's knife.

Two nights prior to the operation, Pooja was suddenly woken from her sleep. Agitated, she looked around her bedroom. It was a clear vision of her father that had interrupted her sleep. In fact, she said out loud, 'Dad, are you here?' But there was no reply.

The next morning, her older son, who was sitting in the hall room finishing his school assignments, suddenly went cold. When asked, he said he had seen *Nana* (maternal grandfather) pacing about in the balcony, dressed in a white kurta-pyjama which was what he typically wore at home when he was alive. The boy had similar visions as a child, soon after his grandfather's demise in 2013. Back then, he would get extremely scared when he saw his grandfather like that, and would scream and cry uncontrollably. He was older now, but it still affected him. Pooja tried to comfort him. But the vision of his Nana's spirit validated her dream. She knew then that her father was still around.

On the morning of the heart surgery, Pooja woke up early and went to the kitchen to prepare breakfast. She let the others sleep a while longer, for she knew what an ordeal the day would be. As she was busy rolling out the dough for the *paratha*s, she was startled when an old Hindi movie song began to play. Then she chuckled at her own overreaction. It was just the radio playing outside. Evidently, her mother had woken up and switched it on.

However, when she came out about 20 minutes later,

hoping to sit with her mother for a while, she was surprised to find that she was still asleep! She went in to check on her sons and they were also asleep. It appeared as if her mother had turned on the radio and then gone back to sleep.

A bit unnerved now, Pooja turned off the radio.

Later, when her mother woke up, Pooja asked her about the radio. The older woman stared at her for a moment, then shook her head. 'I thought *you* had switched on the radio.'

Then there was a sudden moment of realization, and both mother and daughter said at once, 'Dad!'

It was a justified inference. When he was alive, her father was in the habit of listening to Hindi songs on the radio first thing in the morning after waking up.

That realization was the turning point of their day. All the uneasiness that the family had been feeling dissipated. Pooja's mother told her, 'I was afraid of what might happen to me on the operating table today. But now that I know your father is by my side, I feel so much safer.'

Regardless of whether this was true or not, one thing did happen—it boosted the family's confidence. The operation was a success. Everything went back to what it was.

When Sarbajeet was seven years old, his maternal grandmother died of blood cancer. At that time, there was not much awareness of leukaemia, and facilities for treatment were scarce in Bhubaneswar. Her first symptom was bleeding gums, and dark patches appeared all over her skin. Soon, she was deemed blood-deficient. This situation exacerbated to such levels that she needed daily blood transfusions. Sarbajeet's father and uncles were usually the ones who provided her the blood. After a couple of months of living like this, Shakuntala felt a tad better. One evening, she had a long chat with Sarbajeet's mother. After that, she went to bed and never woke up.

In the morning, the family realized that the senior lady had fallen into a coma. She was quickly hospitalized, and that was when it was understood that she had leukaemia. She never woke up from the coma and passed away on the auspicious last day of the Rath Yatra.

However, things did not stop there. Sarbajeet's mother was very close to her mother. She was the youngest and most beloved of her eight children. Her mother's demise, though expected, hit her hard. She did not cry or complain, but withdrew into a shell for a few days. A few days later, she returned to normal life, but things would never be the same again.

From 2005 to 2020, Sarbajeet's mother has reported more than 30 very profound sightings of her mother. She can see her mother quite vividly in her dreams and even in her waking hours. There has never been a moment when she has stopped feeling her presence around her. This could have been dismissed as the psychological response of a grieving daughter, but what is uncanny is the way in which these incidents have at times told her things about her mother that she would never have known otherwise.

In 2011, Sarbajeet's mother fell sick with a viral infection. She had always been a healthy woman who had never even visited a doctor about an illness. Although medicines were prescribed, the virus took its time to leave the body. On the third night of the infection, she developed a high fever. The family members checked on her and let her sleep. Sarbajeet remembers his father sitting up all night, deeply worried. He had decided to take her to a bigger hospital in the city in the morning.

However, at around 3.25 a.m., there was a noise from the room where she had been isolated. Sarbajeet and his father rushed to check on her, and were surprised to find her sitting on the bed. She looked completely normal and was even smiling.

'I saw Ma in my dream,' she said. 'I was madly running towards a cliff. I did not see that I was nearing the edge of the cliff. I stumbled and fell. I was sinking, sinking into the deep ravine below. And just then, I saw something red flying past me. And just like that, I grabbed hold of it. It was the *pallu* (end) of my mother's saree. It was extremely long. I saw her standing on top of the cliff, smiling down at me. She pulled me up with the pallu. The next minute, I was awake.'

It was the strangest of things. The fever was completely gone. In fact, she was suddenly so healthy that she asked for a hearty meal, which was soon provided to her.

This happened again a couple of years later. Her elder brother (Sarbajeet's maternal uncle) had passed away a few years ago. Sarbajeet's mother had been close to him, as was expected of siblings. One night, he came to her in a dream. He invited her to a secret place that she knew of. Fascinated, Sarbajeet's mother began to follow him. But midway there, she saw her own mother (Sarbajeet's grandmother). With an angry look on her face, the older lady scolded Sarbajeet's uncle, 'Why are you taking your sister to that place? Don't you know that she is still a child? Don't ever ask her to come with you like that.'

When Sarbajeet's mother narrated this dream to him, he was quite young to understand it. But in later years he put two and two together. In Hindu belief, when a dead person asks a living person to follow them in a dream, it usually means that the death of the living person is imminent. This is how the dream is interpreted. However, his grandmother's prompt arrival in the dream meant that the time had not yet come.

A few months later, there was an encore to this dream. This time it was about a cousin of Sarbajeet's mother who had died at childbirth many years earlier. In his mother's dream, the cousin promised to take her on a boat ride to the other side of the river. The river was near Sarbajeet's side, the other side of which no one had ever seen. His mother agreed to follow the cousin, but once again it was her mother who intervened. 'She still has a lot of work to do at home. She has to cook for her children. Don't take her on the boat ride now.'

Sarbajeet himself has had one elaborate experience of his *Nani*'s (grandmother) presence in the house. He was studying for his class 12 exams. It was around 2.00 a.m. and he was struggling to grasp a particularly difficult theory. His mind was fully engrossed in the concepts of calculus. Out of the blue, he became aware of the presence of someone standing next to him. Thinking it was his mother checking in on him, Sarbajeet looked up to see her. He was startled to see the form of his grandmother, dressed in the same mud-brown sari that he loved to see on her so much. It appeared to him as if there was a faint smile on her face, just as he remembered from the days when she was alive, and she nodded almost imperceptibly. The most remarkable thing was that she had an aura about her, as if she was radiating some kind of light. Then she disappeared.

The next morning, Sarbajeet's mother told him that she had dreamt of his Nani again. In her dream, she was simply standing and smiling. At that moment, Sarbajeet knew that what he had seen was true. Nani was somehow still in their lives.

And maybe that was a source of reassurance for him. When Sarbajeet's results came out a few weeks later, he had scored well in all the subjects. To this day, he believes that this was on account of his Nani's divine blessing.

Interactive Ghosts and Spirits

We know nothing about the true nature of death, for no one who has gone through the experience has ever come back to tell the tale. What does the act of dying entail? What lies beyond that black curtain of death? Here, we are not talking about the medical symptoms of death; most of us know those. We are talking about death in a spiritual sense. We are talking about the emotional upheavals that affect both the deceased and those who are left behind.

Mourning a loved one's death is one of the biggest challenges to our human emotions. Where does mourning come from? It is essentially a feeling of emptiness, the realization that a person is no longer present in our lives. It is also the fear of not being able to cope with the situation. Not all mourning is selfless. While a lot of people mourn their loved ones because they know they will miss their presence in their lives, a significant number of people also mourn the deceased because the latter was a source of support, and life would be difficult without them.

But these are things that we know. What is not known is whether our mourning makes a difference to the deceased in any way. Do their souls, on their journey through the afterlife, somehow understand the anguish of their bereaved kin who are saddened by their demise? For those who believe in the concept of the soul, this is true. One reason for the elaborate funeral rituals in every religion is to enable the soul to make an unhindered and peaceful journey into the afterlife. But do dead people have any awareness of these rituals? Or, to ask a broader question: are the dead able to see the ones they have left behind, and can they interact with them in some manner?

This leads us to the subject of interactive ghosts.

Across the world, through the ages, and among people of all faiths and religious beliefs, there are countless accounts of people feeling the presence of the departed. Some of these accounts are vague and could be dismissed as unconscious projections of a grieving mind, but there are also accounts that are so overwhelmingly detailed that they cannot be waved away so easily. Especially when the people left behind also have some degree of psychic ability, the feeling of the spiritual presence of the departed is more profound. It may not even be a loved one, but just someone with whom they develop a strong connection.

When the noted singer Céline Dion revealed that she could feel the presence of her husband René Angélil, she was met with a lot of criticism. Céline was married to René for 22 years and there was a strong connection between their souls. She claimed that she not just felt his presence around her, but that she could also talk to him and hear him at times.

The case of Helena Bonham Carter is even more curious. When Bonham Carter was asked to take on the role of Princess Margaret in the third season of the popular show *The Crown*, she wanted to know if she was doing the right thing by portraying a real person who had died. As she revealed at the Cheltenham Literature Festival, Bonham Carter sought the help of a psychic medium, and got in touch with the spirit of Princess Margaret. In Bonham Carter's own words, she heard the soul of the princess tell her that she was glad she would play the role and that she was better than the other actress they were thinking of. Bonham Carter shared that the Princess relayed via the psychic a few instructions on how to approach the role. 'You're going to have to brush up and be neater,' she said, and then said the line that became popular in Hollywood circles, 'Get the smoking right. I smoked in a particular way. Remember that—this is a big note—the cigarette holder was as much a weapon for expression as it was for smoking.'

Theories and Criticism

Even though encounters with ghostly apparitions of loved ones have been widely reported, there are several theories which have tried to explain it. They are more a way to debunk them as normal, rationally explainable phenomena rather than anything paranormal.

The Telepathic Connection

One theory suggests that apparitions are the result of a telepathic connection between the souls of the two people—the deceased and the living. This is believed to be truer in the case of people who die unexpectedly, such as in accidents. Even posthumously, their mind could transmit a telepathic image and appear to someone with whom they have a strong emotional connection.

Such spiritual apparitions, known as *crisis apparitions*, appear to dear ones either at the moment of the person's death or shortly afterwards. Usually, they are forms of expressing gratitude and offering a final goodbye, but at times, they are also known to communicate important details and secrets.

Crisis apparitions, though widely reported, do not generally occur after a particular duration following the person's demise. They are unable to explain how some people can still see the dead years after their departure from the physical world.

Guardian Angels

Some paranormal experts believe in the presence of guardian angels. These are divine entities who govern various aspects of our lives. They are known to help people in difficult times by soliciting divine intervention. In situations where a loved one dies and people are not able to cope with their loss, guardian angels might appear as a spiritual projection of the deceased person. Thus, what the person encounters isn't a 'ghost' of the departed person, but a form that the guardian angel has assumed. They might appear in dreams, which is the most prevalent scenario, or sometimes even manifest as a physical entity. If this is true, it answers the question of why we see the souls of the departed mostly in times of strife.

Hallucinations

The most common theory to explain the apparitions of loved ones or people you have a strong connection with is that they are hallucinations generated by a grieving mind. In times of duress, the brain can produce images of deceased people. These are images of those whom the person banked on or counted on as a source of support during their lifetime.

This theory is the most widely accepted one. Hallucinations are a well-known and medically studied phenomenon. They can explain why people only see the apparitions of certain dead people who were associated with their lives, and not others. Their mind projects the images of only those they feel consoled by in moments of difficulty.

However, due to the transient nature of hallucinations, it is difficult to find evidence of their immediate occurrence.

The truth about seeing the apparitions of loved ones is that they do happen, and till date there is no conclusive theory to explain why. It is a widely discussed subject in paranormal studies, which still stands by the belief that the dead do come back under certain conditions. This is owing to the large number of reported incidents, of which a majority cannot be dismissed with any kind of supposedly logical explanation.

Pooja Vijay saw her deceased father on multiple occasions after his death. Since her father was a spiritual person and her family is spiritually attuned as well, more than one member of her family has seen his apparition, and often their visions have coincided with one another. We conclude with the story of an apparition of her father, which might be one of the most profound experiences any human being has had with the spirit of the deceased.

One night in early March 2020, Pooja was preparing to go to bed. She finished her daily chores and lay down in bed. The day had been full of fun and frolic. The family had dinner together, watched television, and chatted about their plans for the upcoming summer vacation. This year they planned to go to a foreign country they hadn't visited before, and the children were all on board with the idea. It was in such a happy frame of mind that Pooja retired that night.

But no sooner had she hit the bed than she was consumed by a strange feeling. She felt as if she had 'swallowed something cold very quickly' and sat up immediately. There was this sudden cloud of despair that she could feel around her. It was a deeply overwhelming feeling that she had never had before, not even in the extremely haunted places she had visited. She could not sleep easily that night. For a long time, she kept pacing around the room, doing random things and somehow managed to catch a few disturbed moments of sleep.

The feeling persisted the next morning. She still did not know what it was. Was she sick? It didn't feel like something was physically wrong with her. Was her depression from many years ago returning? That also seemed impossible as she had only been in the highest of spirits for the past several months. Things had really been looking up for her.

The family had planned to book the tickets for the expensive foreign vacation that day. But something stopped Pooja from doing so. Despite her sons trying to convince her to book it, all she told them was, 'Let's wait for a couple of days.'

She did not know what was stopping her.

That evening, for some unknown reason, vivid scenes from the day of her father's passing played out in Pooja's mind. She saw him as he lay motionless on the bed where he had been laid. She saw him being decked up for the final procession. A small, long-forgotten memory suddenly came to her mind: her father had predicted his own death a month before he actually died. He had been suffering from cancer for a long time, and his illness had taken a toll on the family. One day in 2013—a day which the family will never forget—he suddenly stirred from his sleep and said, 'Everything will be all right on 20 June.' Pooja's mother asked him what he meant by that, and he simply smiled and said, 'You shall see.' At that time, no one understood the importance of those words. But it was on that day—20 June 2013—that Pooja's father passed away at 5.00 a.m.

Pooja's mother came and sat next to her. 'What happened, Pooja? Are you also feeling uneasy today?'

Pooja perked up and asked, 'Why do you say that, Mom?'

Her mother then told her something that astounded her. 'I don't know what is causing your unease, but since yesterday, I have been having memories of your father. Remember how he kept me from seeing his death that day?'

Pooja had no words. The day had been remarkable for many reasons. Her mother's experience that day was the stuff paranormal movies are made of. It was around 4:50 a.m. Unable to sleep all night, the woman was sitting in her chair, reading something. She decided to go and check on her husband who was in the bedroom. She got up, but before she could take a step, she froze. It was as if something had shackled her feet. She just could not move! Struggling, she somehow doddered back to the chair. She attempted to call out to someone, but the words did not come out. The suffocating feeling persisted for several minutes, and then it suddenly passed. She then immediately rushed into her husband's room, and what did she see but her husband lying still and cold in the bed! With immense grief, she realized what had happened—her husband passed away, but he had also prevented her from seeing the horrific moment of his death.

The rekindling of this memory told Pooja that perhaps her father had returned, as he had done on many other occasions. But she did not know for sure. There was no apparent reason for this. On previous instances, he had come whenever there was a problem looming over the family. However, these were the happiest times possible.

That night, there were more signs of his presence.

There was a photograph of him in the bedroom, which was always garlanded. There was a light next to the frame, which was only lit on special occasions, such as his anniversary or birthday. But on that night, the light came on by itself without any provocation. Pooja entered the room to see the light shining and asked the others about it. No one had switched it on.

As if this weren't enough, there was also an unexpected call from an old friend. Pooja had lost contact with her friend Asmita for many years. The next morning, however, Asmita called and said, 'Pooja, I saw your dad in my dream last night. I don't know why. I haven't thought about him for months. But suddenly he was there, sitting next to me, trying to say something. I was scared and woke up and couldn't go back to sleep again.'

There was also the case of their family cat. This extremely lively pet, went still all of a sudden that evening. He did not respond when he was called. Pooja noticed that he was staring at a particular spot on the big couch in the main hall. That was Pooja's father's favourite spot, where he sat for hours every day, answering his calls. She took a photo of the spot and sent it to Savio, her psychic colleague at PAIRS. Savio got back to her within a few minutes and said, 'Pooja, where is this place? I can see a strong presence at the spot the cat is staring at.'

'Can you describe what you see?' Pooja asked.

A minute later, Savio said, 'It's a slightly dark, hefty man, probably in his sixties.' Pooja was flabbergasted. Savio had never seen her father before. She sent him a photo. In utter disbelief, Savio messaged back, 'This is the man I saw!'

That was all the evidence that was needed to establish that her father had somehow made his presence felt. But what was he trying to say?

The next morning, Pooja's sons reminded her to book the foreign trip. Pooja thought about it. Perhaps this diversion was a good idea. The holidays had already started and people were heading out. Worried that they might be left out for the whole year again, she turned on her laptop. They had already decided everything three days ago; all she had to do was book.

The family sat around the table with great enthusiasm. The boys were the most excited. Pooja checked everything once again and proceeded to the flight-booking website. She filled in the details and after reconfirming everything, she moved her finger to click on the payment button.

And that was when the laptop froze!

It just powered off. Pooja didn't immediately understand what was going on and plugged the charger into the laptop. She knew that laptop was already at more than 50 per cent power, but she plugged it nevertheless. Even then, the laptop wouldn't switch on.

'What's happening, Mom?' her older son said. 'Try your mobile phone.'

Pooja took out the phone. But then she thought for a few minutes and topped. 'No, son. I have a bad feeling about this. I know it's difficult, but let's wait. This laptop thing, it's your Nana's doing, I'm sure of it. He's trying to tell us something. But this might be something that even he doesn't understand and doesn't know how to convey. Let's just wait a few more days, all right?'

Reluctantly, the family decided to wait.

And three days later, they got the answer to their questions.

It was the most bizarre thing imaginable.

It was an announcement by Prime Minister Narendra Modi about the spread of the deadly new coronavirus Covid-19 in India. He announced a one-day lockdown on 22 March as a test and hinted at a longer lockdown thereafter. He spared no words to describe how difficult this pandemic would be and how India was going to battle the virus with all it had.

Perhaps it is too much of a stretch, but even so, the strong sense that Pooja had of her father's spirit being around her, and the many subsequent paranormal events were the reason they did not get stranded abroad during the pandemic. And shortly after they made the decision not to leave, all the paranormal occurrences in the house ceased. Pooja knew then that her father had left. The task he had come for was accomplished.

Sometimes we receive the greatest blessings from our loved ones after they have passed on. But we may need to be receptive when that happens and keep our mind's eye open.

ENCOUNTERS WITH DEATH AND THE AFTERLIFE

Near-Death and Out-of-Body Experiences

'I had seen birth and death but had thought they were different.'

—T.S. Eliot

Asha Lata, Pooja Vijay's aunt, had been suffering from a debilitating sickness for a long time. She had episodes when she would suddenly lose her mind and faint, only to regain consciousness a few minutes later. The disease was chronic; her family could not remember a time when she was not on medication. But everyone in the family had a soft corner for her and volunteered to care for her whenever they could.

On this particular day twenty years ago, it was Pooja's turn to take care of her aunt. Pooja was 20 at the time, still a student but in the middle of a vacation. She was staying at her aunt's house. It was an ordinary summer afternoon. Asha Lata was cleaning her room, following her penchant for tidiness, and Pooja was in the outer room with her little cousin Mayur. Suddenly, they heard a crash from the bedroom. Pooja and Mayur rushed over and found Asha Lata sprawled on the floor.

Pooja did not panic. She reckoned it was another one of her aunt's fainting fits. She knew what had to be done. She tapped on her aunt's shoulder and then on her cheek. She sprinkled some water on her aunt's face. Normally, these practices would bring her back to consciousness, but on this occasion, they did not work. A tad concerned now, Pooja held her finger under her aunt's nose. She could not feel any inhalation or exhalation. Then she tried to feel her pulse, but there was no pulse either. Sensing that this was something she was not equipped to handle, Pooja told Mayur to call his father on the landline phone outside. Mayur rushed out of the room. He dialled the number and called Pooja to the phone when the call was connected.

The call was interrupted by the sound of a loud gasp from the bedroom. Leaving the phone to dangle on its cord, Pooja and Mayur rushed into the bedroom where they saw something that induced both relief and fright at the same time.

Asha Lata was sitting up on the floor, sweating profusely. Her eyes were open, but they appeared to be sightless. There was an expression of utter confusion on her face.

Pooja helped her aunt onto the bed. There was nothing to think about at that point, and no questions were asked. She was just happy that her aunt was alive. She helped her aunt lie down, where she fell asleep almost immediately. Pooja kept a close watch on her as she slept.

That afternoon, Asha Lata slept for two hours straight. After that, she was left to the care of doctors. After a few days of treatment and close observation, the doctors came back with a diagnosis that further surprised everyone. Asha Lata was completely cured of her ailment. There was no way it could have happened. It was a medical miracle.

About a month later, when Asha Lata recovered fully, she began to recount her experience of those few minutes when she had collapsed. She still had a vivid memory of it down to the smallest detail. Fascinated by her experience, Pooja tried to get as much information as she could.

'I remember all of it,' Asha Lata said. 'Every last detail. But I can't describe it fully. There are just no words to explain that sort of thing. Let me try anyway. When I collapsed, the first thing I felt was this sense of incredible lightness. I felt as light as a feather. And I began to float upwards. My senses were completely active and I even tried to call out to you. I could see and hear you. I tried to scream, but no sound escaped my mouth. Then I turned round and saw myself lying on the floor.'

'An out-of-body experience?' Pooja prompted.

'I don't know what you call it. But that sounds about right. I felt as if I had lost my body. I looked down to see my feet, but I didn't see them. I looked at my hands, but they weren't there either. At that moment, I realized that I was bodiless. It was as if I had left my body behind and moved on.'

'How was it when you saw your own body? Was it like seeing yourself in a mirror?' Pooja questioned.

'Not at all!' said Asha Lata. 'In fact, it was quite bizarre. The mirror just duplicates what you do; your reflection is totally in your control. But here my body wasn't in my control. Whatever I did, my body didn't react. I had the uncanny feeling of seeing my body from all sides at the same time—I could see my own back and face from all profiles. That doesn't happen in a mirror.'

'What happened next?' Pooja asked.

'I floated upwards. I don't know where I went, but I rose and rose, and then suddenly found myself in a tunnel. It was very dark now—not like the darkness of the night, but much more intense than that. It was a long, dark tunnel, and it was very straight. Even in the darkness, I could see that.' She paused, as if remembering something. 'And I wasn't alone. Suddenly there were lots of people with me. A big crowd of them, in fact. I had this sense of bonding with them. They were all chatting to one another. Yes, there was a lot of noise. Everyone was talking at the same time. But do you know what the strangest thing was? Nobody moved their mouths. The voices were just there.'

'Telepathic communication?' said Pooja.

Asha Lata went on, ignoring the jargon. 'We were all moving in the forward direction. No one told me which way to go, but I just knew. It was like standing in a queue for something. But there were also people moving outside the queue. And there...' She drew in a deep sigh and rubbed her arms because she was breaking out into goosebumps. '... I saw them all. My family. My mother was there, and she was standing with Hari Uncle.'

'Your mother? Hari Uncle? But they are...' Pooja said.

'Yes. Dead. For a long time. But I saw them. They were happy. They were gesturing to me. It was a sign of reassurance that everything would be all right.'

'How did you feel?' asked Pooja.

'Happy. Very happy. I had absolutely no pain. This throbbing in my chest, it wasn't there at all. I didn't even have a heart. No heartbeat, no pulse. It was the most incredible feeling. I was so free, so much at peace, that I cannot describe it at all.'

'What was going on? Where did everyone go?' Pooja asked.

'Yes, I am coming to that. So, ahead of us, as the queue moved further, I realized that there was a kind of door frame. It was a gigantic doorway with a bright white light shining through it. Now, I saw light, but it was unlike any light we've seen on earth. It was so, so dazzling that I could not bear it, even though I had no eyes. I don't know if "blinding" is the right word, but that is what it was. Everyone moved towards this light, one by one. They passed through the door frame and then vanished. It was like diving into a fabulous swimming pool.'

'I've heard of such lights when...'

'No, no one can understand it. I tell you, this was something else. I was drawn to it like a moth to a flame. The attraction was immense.'

'What happened then?'

'I was just about to reach the light, and I was so eager to just pass through, when I heard a voice. It was just a voice; I don't know who had spoken. But it gives me such goosebumps even to think of it. Look!'

'What did the voice say?'

'It asked me, "It's not your time. Do you still want to go?" I was stunned for a second. Although there were so many people there, I knew it was me who had been asked this question. In a flash, my consciousness took a different direction. Suddenly I was reminded of my life here on earth. Everything flashed through my mind in just a matter of seconds—my life, from my birth up to that point. And of all that, one thing stood out. It was Mayur's face. I could easily have walked through it (believe me, the temptation was strong) but I had one chance. It was not my time. I didn't want to leave Mayur alone. I found myself shaking my head and saying "no".'

'Oh...then?'

'Then I woke up here. I heard the loud gasp that left my body. My eyes opened. Suddenly I could see. I felt the weight of my body. I sat up and realized that even that took so much effort. For a moment, I did not understand where I was. I was disorientated. That was when you came and caught hold of me.'

No one spoke for a while after that. Asha Lata had said everything she wanted to say. Then Pooja worked a smile on her face and asked her aunt to relax. 'Thanks for sharing your experience. But now you must rest. We're all so happy that you are hale and hearty.'

When Pooja narrated Asha Lata's experience to me, I had no reservations in my mind that it was true. However, it is possible that she had exaggerated some of the details. I have noticed that this is true when people are recounting experiences that they don't understand. In narrating them, they are prone to add details that perhaps did not occur, but seem true to them in retrospect. For me, as an author chronicling these paranormal experiences of various people, it is a challenge to sift the real from the supposed, so I stick to reproducing their narrations as I received them and leave it to my readers to assess them.

Pooja fully understood and related with her aunt's experience. In parapsychology, this is called a near-death experience, abbreviated as NDE. She did not spell that out to her aunt exactly because she did not want to alarm her with the D-word. But if Pooja had been more experienced at the time, she would have realized that the D-word wouldn't worry her aunt anymore. For, Asha Lata, like most people who have had a near-death experience, isn't afraid of death anymore.

Near-Death Experience

A near-death experience is an experience wherein a person feels that they have ceased to physically exist and are moving towards an afterlife, only to be brought back to the physical world. The entire experience usually lasts only a few minutes and occurs in people who have fatal illnesses, been through a serious accident, or are in a state of deep meditation.

Near-death experiences are a very common phenomenon, so common, in fact, that specific patterns thereof have been studied. Hospitals abound with stories of patients who have seen the 'white light at the end of the tunnel', and have come back. Often, these are patients who are suffering from fatal illnesses or who have been involved in serious accidents. In the few minutes that these patients are gone, they are reported as clinically dead. However, defying all explanations, these people return and have stories to tell.

In recent times, near-death experiences have gained a lot of credence when famous personalities have come forward and shared their own experiences. One widely discussed experience is that of American actress Sharon Stone. Stone suffered a subarachnoid brain haemorrhage in 2001. The doctors did all they could, but at some point they feared that they couldn't do anything more. Stone realized that. While in the MRI machine, she saw the look of helplessness on her doctor's face. But once she was inside, she had a completely different experience.

As she recounted on an episode of Oprah Winfrey's show and the American magazine *Closer*, Stone felt as if she was being pulled into a giant vortex of white light. She saw people around her; they were her friends and relatives who had already passed away. She had the knowledge and awareness that she was dead and she was moving towards a glorious white light. She also speaks of a journey in which she was taken to places 'both here and beyond'. This could be the experience of life flashing by, which many people who have had NDEs have spoken of. The whole episode lasted a couple of minutes, after which she was back in her body and breathing again.

What Stone also recounts—and is important for us to note—is that she had an incredible sense of well-being. Death did not frighten her at all; rather, she describes it as a gift and a glorious, beautiful thing. She also has a take on death that hasn't been spoken of before—that death is very close to us, that it is right around the corner, and that there's no need to fear it because it is very safe.

Another lucid account of a near-death experience

was that of Bryce Bond, an American media personality who, in his later years, turned into a parapsychologist. A violent allergic reaction to pine nuts had caused him to be hospitalized. This is where he had his NDE, which he chronicled in his book *Beyond the Light*. Here he describes the tunnel and the white light, as most patients with NDEs have done, but he also speaks specifically about his pet dog. It was his black poodle named Pepe, who had passed away a few years ago. As he was approaching the white light, the poodle came racing towards him, and it triggered a great emotional surge. Bond describes that at that moment, he felt that the poodle was even more real than it had been in life, and he felt a much stronger bond with his pet than ever before. He could even sense the animal's great joy at being reunited with him.

Bond goes on to explain further that he found it hard to turn back when he heard the voice saying to him, 'It's not your time.' He had experienced such profound joy and peace in these short moments that he did not want to return to the world of pain. He describes the feeling of not wanting to return as 'overwhelming'. But when he did come back, which he physically felt by the prick of a hypodermic needle in his arm, he heard the words 'welcome back'. However, no one in the hospital care unit where he was being treated had uttered these words.

Similarities in Near-Death Experiences

In studying thousands of NDEs from all over the world and across the ages, many common patterns have been observed.

1. Everyone who has gone through a near-death experience speaks of a long dark tunnel and a kind of white light at its end. At least the light is always a factor, and it appears in different forms. Some people have claimed to be sucked in by the light, while others have felt uncontrollably drawn to it but never seemed to reach it.
2. There is also always the presence of people who have passed away and were close to the person in their lifetime. These could be close friends, teachers, or relatives—usually people who are still missed by the person having the NDE. In certain cases, people have also seen their pets, their idols and role models who have passed on.
3. NDEs usually happen to people who die tragically, such as after prolonged illnesses or serious accidents. The number of NDEs is higher among younger people who die unexpectedly than it is among older people. Sometimes they are also experienced by people who practise deep meditation. In such cases, it could be said that an NDE can be induced.
4. People who have NDEs come out feeling deeply spiritual and religious afterwards. They start believing in the existence of god (if they were not believers before), and their outlook towards life changes. Many people have said after a NDE that death is nothing to be afraid of. They speak of the beauty of death. They talk about the moment when they were told that it was not their time, and they invariably said that they didn't want to come back to the world of pain, but had to because of the people they had left behind or

they still had not fulfilled their purpose in life.

5. There is also a heightened feeling of 'self' among people who have had an NDE. They talk about how, during the experience, they felt as if they were the centre of the universe, as if everything revolved around them. They also talk about how their self was filled with love and compassion and that these were the only things that mattered in the final reckoning with the universe. People who have come back appreciate life more, and they turn kinder and more compassionate in the second phase of their lives.

Out-of-Body Experience

An out-of-body experience occurs when a person has the momentary sense that they are outside their physical bodies, and can see their physical bodies from an external frame of reference. It ends when the person finds themselves back in their bodies.

An out-of-body experience is one step lower than a near-death experience because there is no brush with death. It is one's temporary departure from the corporal form, only to return to it a few minutes later. No one knows what brings about an out-of-body experience, although some claim that deep meditation can trigger it.

Ritu Lalit, a popular deep meditator and author of the book *From Son to Stranger*, has described multiple out-of-body experiences. She puts it thus, 'I was meditating out in the open and I just shot out [of my body] and the view was awesome. All of a sudden, I was out in the tree. I sat on the ground under a tree and leaned against it.

In the distance, I heard drums. It was the youth festival in a college, and they were playing some folk tunes. I felt the beats synchronizing with my heartbeats and the rhythm of my body. Then I saw a form of energy. It was neon blue, almost white, and it connected me with the trees, the grass, the stars, and the moon. I felt the entire experience to be an energy link to the cosmos.'

Lalit, who describes herself as a habitual meditator, says that she triggers out-of-body experiences for herself to regain her sanity. She describes the feeling as 'trippy' and says, 'in that moment I was everything, everything was me.'

Out-of-body experiences are an isolated phenomenon, and not everyone has them voluntarily. For most, these experiences are triggered for unknown reasons, but they leave behind a supreme sense of self. Pooja's aunt Asha Lata describes her out-of-body experience as follows, 'When I could see my own body from the outside, I realized what a small, insignificant thing I was. All that really matters is our spiritual form, which you might call soul or *aatma*. We read in our scriptures that our body is but a vessel. But it is the people who have gone through near-death and out-of-body experiences who will really tell you how insignificant this vessel is. Our holy men who can easily induce out-of-body experiences know of this insignificance, and that is why they do not attach great importance to the material form of our existence. That is also why they do not consider death to be the end. Knowing these two facts and sensing them for real is a truly liberating experience.'

We conclude with an experience recounted by Sarbajeet

Mohanty, who has himself had both out-of-body and near-death experiences. It was an experience that changed his perspective on life, and made him the person he is today.

It happened during one of his first meditation sessions. He had just started meditating and was experiencing the serenity of it in his room with no one around him. There was nothing to distract him. It was only him and his thoughts, and then the thoughts began to recede. Soon he felt the thoughts beginning to dissolve into a kind of vortex, and he felt himself being pushed into it. At this time, his mind seemed to have gained a life of its own. He allowed himself to be pulled into the vortex and it led him to a place and a dimension he had never been to before.

He saw a long, narrow and dark tunnel in front of him.

Having studied the experiences of others, the conscious part of his mind knew where he was. Still, he could not stop himself from walking into the tunnel. It was a strange gait, though. He glided along, no part of his body touching any surface, for he had no body at all. He had transcended into his spiritual form. Then he came to the light.

The light was brilliant and blinding, and at the same time, soothing and peaceful. He was fascinated by how awe-inspiring it was. It obliterated everything he had in mind in the first instance that he saw it. He felt the unstoppable urge to keep on moving towards it. He had a deep sense of being liberated and he knew this feeling would be irrevocable once he crossed the light, and he kept moving towards it until he almost touched it.

But it was then that he heard the voice—a deep masculine voice—that clearly told him, 'Not your time'.

That was all he heard. The next moment, he opened his eyes and was back in his room.

Sarbajeet's experience changed him in several ways. Most notably, it started him on this journey with the paranormal. He says that this experience has enabled him to have a better understanding of people. For example, he can now recognize when a person is lying to him. All of us have this ability to some extent, but he can understand it on a deeper level. He has started disliking crowds because he is affected by the multiple auras that such places radiate. His experience also had several positive effects. He can now connect more deeply with people who are on the same wavelength as him. And, most importantly, like others who have gone through these experiences, Sarbajeet has developed a strong sense of kindness and compassion, and has come to understand that empathy and love are the only things that really matter in the overall scheme of things in this beautiful universe we live in.

GAMES OF THE DEAD

Ouija Boards

'It's not so important who starts the game, but who finishes it.'

—John Wooden

Fraternal twins Santosh and Priyanka discovered something interesting while cleaning the junk from the attic of their cottage in a small town in central India. Years ago, they had made it as a toy to play with just for fun. Now, it had come back to haunt them, as such things are wont to do. This object was a shoddy replica of a Ouija board. The rudimentary board they had amateurishly assembled contained all the necessary elements on a piece of plywood—the letters of the alphabet, the words 'yes', 'no', 'hello', and 'goodbye', and the planchette. They had built it exactly as they had seen it in their favourite horror films. However, their excitement was confined to its creation. They had never felt the inclination to play with it. Or, to put it rightly, an unspoken fear kept them from tinkering with the device they had manufactured.

Just like all those years ago, they decided to put it

away unused this time as well. They were in their twenties now. They had better sense now, and they ought to have discarded the board altogether, but they didn't. It was a source of nostalgia.

Then, two years later, they came across the board again. Like a bad penny, it refused to go away. This time they didn't just stuff it away. There was a tragic development in their family that made them reconsider it. The twins had lost their beloved grandfather a few weeks ago. Dadaji had showered all his love on them, and his sudden demise had plunged them into a state of gloom. Neither of them had managed to come out of that deep personal loss.

'What if we try it just once?' Santosh uttered the words that were on Priyanka's mind as well.

After much deliberation, the two of them decided to go ahead. What did they have to lose anyway? If the Ouija board did not work, so be it. And if it did, they would have a chance to speak to their Dadaji. Thus, the two of them sat down on the floor and laid the board out between them. It was two in the afternoon. Only their mother was at home. She was in her room taking a nap. The siblings looked at each other and exchanged a gesture of reassurance. Then, as they had seen in the horror movies, they held the planchette together.

They began with 'hello', and Santosh said in the local dialect of Odia that was spoken in the house, 'Dadaji, if you are here and see us, please accept our greeting. We just want to talk to you.'

There was a long moment of silence. Nothing happened.

'If you are here, Dadaji, please give us a sign,' Priyanka

said, her eyes brimming with tears. 'We miss you so much!'

This went on for a while. The teenagers asked questions hoping for the planchette to show some signs of movement at least, but nothing happened. Eventually, they realized that this was an exercise in futility, and decided to stop. To do that, they knew they had to first bid the spirit goodbye, which meant moving the planchette from its blank position on the word 'Goodbye'. Holding it together, the two of them started to move the planchette. That was when they had the first sign that something was off.

'It's not moving!' Priyanka exclaimed. 'Are you doing something?'

'No!' said Santosh, bewildered.

The planchette was moving weirdly. Stuck in its position, it was now rapidly vibrating to and fro.

'What are you two doing?' A voice sounded from behind them. Their mother had come into the room. She looked curiously at the board. 'What is that?'

Thankfully for the twins, their mother had no idea what a Ouija board was.

'It's just a game, Ma! We're just putting it away,' Priyanka said, and they quickly let go of the planchette. And then their mouths fell open.

The moment they let go of the planchette, there was a scraping sound. They looked down at the board and saw—the planchette was moving of its own free will.

The twins were so horrified by this movement—and also because they didn't want their mother to see it—that they quickly shoved the board back into the attic.

A week passed and neither of them spoke about the Ouija board. Santosh was the one thinking about it more because in addition to everything that had happened on the board, he had also sensed something moving in the room. He was so freaked out by it that he did not dare enter the room, or check the attic where they had kept the board.

And then his terror rose to new heights when Priyanka fell ill.

It began as a slight temperature in the afternoon, which, by evening, graduated to a state of delirium. Priyanka suddenly stopped responding, she was so emaciated. Her mother gave her some home remedies and managed to bring the fever down. The next day, however, the fever returned, so the family decided to take her to the doctor. The doctor checked her, advised the family not to worry as it was a normal fever, and sent them back with some antibiotics.

Despite all this, Santosh was in a terrible state. He was sure that his sister's fever was not ordinary. There was something bizarre going on. Though he suspected he was simply overthinking and letting his imagination run riot, he could swear that at times he saw a shadow-like glitch in the house, especially in his sister's room when no one was around.

He was petrified and didn't know whom to talk to. There was no doubt in his mind that they had unleashed something that day, and that was the source of their problems.

It was two weeks into Priyanka's illness that Santosh came to the PAIRS office with his bizarre story. In one breath, he told Sarbajeet and Pooja everything that had happened and requested them to come to the house and examine his sister's condition.

From the pictures of the house that the PAIRS team observed, it could be assessed that something was different about it. Santosh led them to his sister's room. She was in a state of semi-consciousness and was unable to speak. The family asserted that her condition was beyond the ken of medical knowledge. After this preliminary assessment, an elaborate investigation needed to be conducted.

Using her psychic abilities, Pooja surveyed the house and determined that there was indeed some negative energy in the house. It was localized around Priyanka, but she could not say with conviction what exactly it was.

Next, Sarbajeet checked the surroundings with the K2 meter. There was no abnormal activity throughout the house, but the moment he stepped into Priyanka's room, he got an unusual reading. The meter was erratic, with up to three lights blinking[6]. He stepped out and went back inside. When he left the room, the lights went back to normal, but lit up when he returned. This indicated the presence of an intense electromagnetic field in the room. The team had rarely observed such consistency in readings on any previous occasion.

This was all the evidence the paranormal investigators needed to establish that there was something unnatural in the room. The twins' parents were apprised of the situation and their permission was sought to perform a cleansing ritual. The PAIRS team performed a specific spirit-cleansing ritual using salt-water and an herb called California sage. The ritual lasted a couple of hours. The

---

[6]In usual conditions, only one light stays steadily on.

entire time the ritual was being performed, Priyanka stayed in a semi-conscious state, dazed by what was happening around her.

Two hours after the completion of the ritual, the room was checked again with the K2 meter. This time, the device had gone back to normalcy. Satisfied with what they had done, Sarbajeet and his team bid goodbye and left.

Sarbajeet followed up with the family a week later. He was happy to see that they appeared much at ease. Priyanka was sitting upright and talking. Her fever had subsided, though she still bore the weakness of a recuperating patient. There were a number of medicines on her bedside table. They believed that the doctors had finally cured her of her prolonged sickness, but Santosh told Sarbajeet in confidence that she showed signs of recovery soon after the ritual.

Then Santosh asked a question that had been plaguing him for a long time, 'But, Sarbajeet bhaiya, was the spirit you identified in the house our Dadaji's? How could he harm Priyanka? He loved her so much. Why would he make her sick?'

Sarbajeet had not expected this question. 'So you think it was your Dadaji's spirit?'

'Wasn't it him?'

'There was a presence in your house, but it was definitely not your Dadaji,' Sarbajeet explained. 'It was something else, something harmful and vicious. Your sister was in the clutches of this malevolent entity. We tried to communicate with it, but it wouldn't respond. But its vengeance was not against your sister, so it was easy to remove it from her.'

'Then how did it get into our house?' Santosh asked.

'One cannot say for sure, but it's easy to think that your little tryst with the Ouija board might have had something to do with it.'

Santosh's face contorted. 'It was all my mistake. I pushed her to play with the Ouija board.'

'Look, Santosh, don't beat yourself about it. The Ouija board is just a toy. If you know its history, you'll see that it's nothing more than a plaything. This piece of wood can't help you communicate with the other side. But that doesn't mean that there isn't an "other side". There are spirits all around us, good ones and bad ones. And when you start playing with such devices, you are, in fact, giving those spirits a signal that you are weak and vulnerable, that you are willing to accept them in your home. That's why they came to you. The board does nothing really, but it's the very act of playing with it that does the harm.'

'So it was not my Dadaji for sure?'

'A hundred times sure. It was something else that was around and latched on to you because you were so needy. It took advantage of you. Stay away from the board. Destroy it, in fact.'

'That's another thing,' Santosh said slowly. 'I wanted to burn that damned board when Priya fell sick. Somehow I gathered the courage to go to the attic. But the board wasn't there. I looked and looked, but it had vanished. Do you think...?'

'Ah, look closely,' Sarbajeet said. 'Maybe you have just misplaced it.'

Sarbajeet walked away, but now he had an odd

sensation that something was still amiss. Ouija boards don't vanish just like that. But he didn't want to alarm the family any further. He resigned himself to the fact that though we know a lot about this world, there is still an infinite number of things that remains unknown.

Ouija Board

After hearing the curious case of the twins, Sarbajeet and I settled down to a conversation about the Ouija board. How is it that a simple device made on a basic wooden board can captivate the attention of the entire paranormal world? To explain this, let me take you through the history of the Ouija board.

It might surprise many to know that the Ouija board, which has become such a mainstay of horror lore, was actually designed as a toy by a company called the Kennard Novelty Company in America in 1891. At the time, Americans were deeply involved in various spiritual practices. Séances were quite common, even as a parlour game at the parties of the elite. It was a time of war and strife, and people looked for these séances as a way to communicate with the dead.

During this time, an entrepreneur named Charles Kennard saw a great money-making opportunity. Until then, séances were just performed by sitting around and talking. Kennard came up with the idea of providing these séances with a device or tool that people could play with. It would also give these sessions a unique identity.

There was already a basic version of the device known as the 'spirit board' or 'talking board', but it had not gained any popularity. Kennard took the idea and redesigned it on a wooden board, incorporating the design of the two semi-circular arcs consisting of the letters of the English alphabet, the numbers 1 to 10 and the four words—'yes', 'no', 'hello' and 'goodbye'. He then got a rich businessman named Elijah Bond, and a few others to invest in the Kennard Novelty Company, and the first version of the board was developed. It was marketed as a board that could aid communication with spirits, and given the sentiment in America at the time, it gained immense popularity in no time.

The story behind the naming of the Ouija board is as mysterious as the board itself. One popular legend says that the name comes from none other than the board itself. When Kennard and a group of friends were thinking about what they should call the board, almost immediately, the planchette spelled out the letters O-U-I-J-A. There are many theories about how this must have happened. It is possible that the name was inspired by the then-popular feminist author Ouida, whose image was on a locket worn by one of the participants in this session—Helen Peters, who was Bond's sister-in-law and claimed to be a strong medium. However, many critics debunk this theory stating that it was put forth by the marketing team to lend credibility to the board, and in fact, the name was just inspired by combining the words 'oui' and 'ja' for 'yes' in French and German respectively.

There is an even more curious story about how the patent was obtained for the Ouija board. When they presented their case, the patent officer was understandably reluctant to grant them a patent. Upon their insistence, the officer asked the group to demonstrate the Ouija board's capabilities. The condition he laid down was simple: 'If the board spells out my first name, I will allow the patent to proceed.' Helen Peters interrogated the board, and soon enough the officer's first name was spelt out as clear as day! This shook the officer so much that he immediately allowed the patent to go through.

However, even this story is discredited by sceptics. The justification given is that Bond was a frequent visitor at patent offices, and it is very possible that he already knew the patent officer's name beforehand.

Be that as it may, the Ouija board is here to stay. Today, its popularity has spread all over the world, and it's not just confined to parlour games. The board has almost become an icon of horror memorabilia. Some of the earliest boards have attained the stature of valuable antiques. Entire movies and web-series are made on the concept of Ouija boards, which have fuelled their popularity. At horror conventions and meetings, it is common to see different variations of the Ouija board being used by people with great deal of anticipation.

However, the debate is still on as to whether there is any credibility to these boards. Apart from being an interesting game, are these boards really a medium to get through to the other side and communicate with spirits? People are divided in their opinions.

How Do Ouija Boards Work?

To understand how the Ouija board works, we must first consider a biological sensory phenomenon known as the ideomotor effect. This is a neuropsychological effect whereby a person makes physical movements without being aware of it. These movements are effected by the agency of the brain, which sends the impulses to the motor nerves without the involving the sensory nerves. This way, it is a reflex action that only involves a muscular output (movement) without any sensory input.

When we perform a task over and over again, it is often so strongly registered in our brain that the action occurs even without any conscious thought. Consider an action like switching on the lights when entering a dark room. Or waving your hand at a friend you see in the street. Or, talking in a cute voice in the presence of an infant. These actions aren't assigned to us by our conscious mind. We just do them because we have been doing them forever, and now these responses are ingrained in our muscle memory.

The Ouija board works in a similar fashion. One of the most credible theories to explain its action is that the person using the board already has the desired answers in their memory. The ambience of a séance is such that the person is in a trance-like state, and not fully conscious of their actions. This is when the motor nerves take over and move the fingers with the help of muscle memory in accordance with the person's stored memory. This, in turn, makes the user move the planchette. When this works, the planchette moves to the desired locations on the board. So if a person really desires to communicate with a deceased person, their fingers will unconsciously spell out the person's name on the board.

This is not cheating, per se. The ideomotor effect is an involuntary action, that is, an action that is not consciously willed. The people handling the planchette are not conscious that they are moving their fingers, and therefore the responses that appear on the board shock them.

Sarbajeet explains this with an example. 'A lady once visited us with the request to be put in contact with her dead husband. Even ten years after his demise, she still loved her husband dearly. During the conversation, she mentioned his name 'Nimesh' scores of times as if he were still alive. We did not want to work with her on the Ouija board, but she was adamant. In fact, she had even brought her own board. We finally agreed to do it. But it was soon clear that the woman was moving the planchette herself. For a while, we thought she was tricking us. But it was not a trick. Her fingers were moving on their own, jumping up to the desired replies. She also spelt his name—N-I-M-E-S-H. Her joy at each of these answers was genuine. That was when we knew how a Ouija board really works at a psychological level. This woman was not psychotic. The only thing that stood out about her was that she was still deeply attached to her husband and felt his presence around her. We bade goodbye to her without bursting her bubble. It seemed like she needed this moment of joy. But we did caution her not to use the Ouija board when she was alone and told her about its dangerous effects.'

Sarbajeet recounted another recent Ouija board-related case in Mumbai. This, by his own admission, was a truly bizarre and hair-raising case. It was the case of Paridhi Nayak, a 19-year-old college student who reported the presence of an old, hunchbacked lady in a red sari in her room. Paridhi's family was well-to-do and lived in a bungalow. While the upper floor was occupied by her parents, her bedroom was on the ground floor of the house.

Her visions had started a year ago. It started when she began to hear noises in the kitchen next to her room at night. At first she would think it was her mother. But she was shocked when she found a few days later that it wasn't her mother; in fact, her mother thought that it was her pottering around in the kitchen for late-night snacks. After this realization, the noises from the kitchen stopped, but other things started to happen. One morning she woke up and saw a trail of muddy footprints leading from the door to her bedroom window. This freaked her out.

Then it occurred to her that the culprit was a Ouija board that she and a group of friends had played with a few weeks ago. Just for kicks, they had tried calling the spirit of their professor named Sulabha, who had recently passed away. Nothing had happened at that point, but now Paridhi was almost sure that they had summoned something. She called her friends to express her fears. They initially sympathized with her but then strangely stopped talking to her, as if they didn't want to be affected by whatever was happening to her.

Meanwhile, the hunchbacked woman grew more and more sinister with each passing night. One night, Paridhi woke up to the sound of her name being called and had a momentary vision of the woman standing by the side of her bed. She refuted it then, wishing it away as an illusion.

But, a few nights later, as she prepared to lie down to sleep, she felt as if someone was in her bed. Imagine her horror when she lifted the cover and saw the body of the old, hunchbacked woman lying crumpled in the sheets. Again, it was over in a flash, but it made her heartbeat soar to near explosion.

When Paridhi's parents came to know about this, they wasted no time in trying everything they could to resolve the issue. They started with the usual measures—calling a holy man, reading from the scriptures, conducting a *havan* in the house, and performing every ritual supposed to ward off spirits. But the presence did not let off.

Paridhi's health began to deteriorate. She would not be able to sleep entire nights, and on the rare occasion when she did, she would wake up to creepy sounds, and once even with strange marks on her body. This physical affliction was the strongest manifestation of the paranormal presence in her life.

It was at this point that the family consulted Sarbajeet. The Ouija board was mentioned right at the outset. Since Sarbajeet had prior experiences with people dabbling with Ouija boards, he was prepared. A presence was indeed detected in the house. Not just that, Sarbajeet, with the help of his team, could pinpoint exactly who this spirit was.

It was the spirit of a beggar lady who spent all her time at a traffic light near their house. The lady had died in her sleep on the footpath about seven years ago. Her spirit was still believed to move about in the vicinity, looking for an adequate place to make her new home. She had probably taken the Ouija board as a kind of invitation. Everything now fell into place.

The spirit was located with great difficulty and dispensed with, and an elaborate cleansing ritual was performed. The team waited a few days and visited the family again. The family reported that there were no further untoward incidents happening in the house. But Paridhi said that even though she did not see the old lady anymore, she felt her presence around her, and that she wished her grave harm.

At this point, Sarbajeet knew that Paridhi's ailment was also related to psychological factors. It was decided that since it had started with a Ouija board, it had to end with it. A Ouija board was procured and this time, under careful supervision, Paridhi was asked to send the spirit away by saying 'goodbye'. The whole family watched with great amazement as the girl's hands moved the planchette to the 'goodbye' position, seemingly without the application of her conscious mind. And the sordid affair came to an end.

However, it took Paridhi years to come out of this harrowing experience. She had been mentally traumatized by the whole chain of events. She failed her final exams that year. She also went through an extremely painful break-up, which exacerbated the issue. More than the presence of the spirit, it was the after-effects of the haunting in various facets of her life that jeopardized her career and relationships. She would regret that one careless moment of dabbling with the Ouija board for years to come.

Even though the entire paranormal fraternity may be divided over the issue of Ouija boards, Sarbajeet has been quite upfront about it. He is of the firm opinion that the board itself is nothing more than a toy. In his words, 'A piece of wood or plastic with the alphabet and numbers on it cannot be considered to be a portal to the other world. It makes no sense. The Ouija board was invented to be a game and that is what it is.'

His experience comes from all the cases he has investigated so far, where the board did not do what its users hoped it would. In addition to this, he believes that the movement of the planchette is merely a result of the ideomotor reflex; there is nothing otherworldly about that particular aspect of the board.

However, it is also true that people have suffered from grave consequences after handling the board. Given the emotional state of most people who play with a Ouija board, it makes them vulnerable, and that is what these entities feed on. These entities are all around us. We cannot see them because of our human limitations. But when someone dabbles with a device like a Ouija board, they are in fact sending a message that they are open to be played with. And that is where all hell quite literally breaks loose. This is clearly proved by the fact that sceptics never see anything happen when dealing with a Ouija board, and they will not suffer any consequences either.

Sarbajeet puts it like this, 'The spiritual world is like an invisible marketplace teeming with spirits. They are all around us, but we cannot see them. Using the Ouija board is like calling these spirits, and it is quite possible that one of them heeds the call and crosses over.'

Things like the Ouija board are best left as they are. Though the board might itself be innocent, we know almost nothing about the world on the other side. Using the board might just be the invitation the other side needs to cross over to ours, and it's best not to extend such an invitation to them.

THE NOISY GHOSTS

Poltergeists

'I've never seen a poltergeist, but I do believe that there is more than what we see, and more than just this.'

—Timothy Spall

This incredibly hair-raising case is sourced from the old case files of the Parapsychology and Investigations Research Society (PAIRS).

It was the November of 2016. Diwali had just got over and the nationwide festivities had come to an end. The PAIRS office had resumed their work after a short break. On one of these days, a woman in her thirties walked into the office without an appointment. She asked to meet Pooja Vijay and was brought into her room.

This woman was Varsha Mathur, an old acquaintance of Pooja's. As she looked around the office, she sat down heavily on a chair and wiped the sweat off her brow. She recounted how she had been trying to get in touch with her over the Diwali holidays, and had somehow managed to locate her office address. Having dispensed with these initial greetings, she got straight down to her order of business.

Without mincing her words, Varsha explained that someone had put a hex on her family and had completely destabilized their lives. The case had to do with Varsha's parents' house, which was located in Borivali, a northern suburb of Mumbai. The house was an apartment in a 40-year-old building. Her parents and her unmarried elder brother lived in this house. They had lived there peacefully for many years, but just two months before Diwali, curious things had started happening in the house.

It all started when Varsha's father, a septuagenarian, suddenly collapsed one evening. He was a healthy and active man, and very particular about his diet and fitness. It came as a bit of a shock when the diagnosis stated that he had a heart attack. Even the doctors were puzzled because the man was healthy in all aspects. Almost overnight, Varsha's father went from being an energetic jogger who walked three kilometres a day to a bedridden old man.

This abrupt change in the family's routine was followed by several bizarre incidents that took place in the old apartment. About a week after Varsha's father collapsed, her mother tripped and fell in the corridor of the house. She was not injured but badly shaken. When anyone asked her how she fell, she replied, 'Someone caught my feet and deliberately tripped me.' She was willing to wager that someone had done it, and that after she fell, she heard someone chuckling. She immediately turned around to look, but she couldn't see anyone.

This led to a string of eerie things happening in and around the house. What really shook them was the fact that the faucets of the house would turn on by themselves. They would run on their own at night after everyone had gone to bed. The water would noisily pour out until the sinks overflowed. At first, the Mathurs thought that someone was leaving the faucets open by mistake, but when it started happening in the middle of the day too, there was no doubt that something very sinister was at work.

Five days before Diwali, Saurabh, Varsha's older brother, was sitting in his room and reading. Suddenly he was startled beyond belief. He saw someone walk past the door of his room. It was a very quick movement that neither his mother nor his father could have managed. It appeared as if a child had run past him, making a funny sound. Nevertheless, he called out to his mother to ask her if it was her. There was no response. He came out into the corridor to find that his mother was asleep in her room.

And that was not the only time this happened. Over the next few weeks, every member of the family sensed a mysterious being in the house. Most curiously, this being did not try to hide. It walked past them in the centre of the room or hid behind a door and disappeared as soon as someone entered a room. Once Mrs Mathur walked into the kitchen to see, out of the corner of her eye, something sitting on the top shelf. When she looked, it had disappeared.

The brunt of all this was borne by the old father. Being sick and mostly confined to his bed, he was particularly vulnerable to the haunting. He would wake up at night hearing strange noises in his room. Once he found his medicine strewn on the floor. Another time, a chair in his room had tipped over. Sometimes, his blanket would move by itself, especially at night when he was asleep, leaving him cold and shivering.

Most of these strange noises originated in the kitchen. Initially, the Mathurs thought that someone was in the kitchen, but it was soon established that even when there was no one there, the clattering of pots and pans could be heard from the rest of the house. Such things became a regular occurrence in the house.

Varsha recounted these incidents in detail for over two hours. When she was done, she leaned forward as if revealing a big secret. 'So this is it, Pooja, Sarbajeet. This is what is going on in my house. My poor father won't be able to take it much longer, I am afraid. And the thing is: I know why this is happening. Someone has put a hex on my father. He made a lot of enemies in his business.'

Pooja and Sarbajeet did not want to commit to anything without first visiting the house. It was a serious allegation—blaming someone of having hexed a family, and adequate research was needed. More than anything, the strictly physical nature of most of the bizarre things that were happening in the house piqued their curiosity. They bade Varsha Mathur goodbye, but assured her that they would soon make an appointment to visit the house.

The case had all the promise of turning out to be a special investigation. So far, they had to cajole ghosts to make an appearance. But this mischievous entity loved to make itself known with much noise and fanfare.

The investigation was scheduled three days later. Sarbajeet and Pooja arrived at the apartment at the right time. As expected, it was in an old building that had not been renovated since it was built. The exterior paint of the building had fully weathered away over the years. The garden in the building grounds looked as if it had never been tended. The building had no elevator. When the investigators went up the stairs, they found that almost all the steps were broken and chipped. Everything around it was in poor, neglected state—exactly the kind of place that could be a favorite habitat for unseen entities.

The team set to work. Sarbajeet started with the faucets of the house. There were five faucets in the house, all of which he duly checked. Nothing seemed to be functionally wrong with them—the taps were secure and there were no leaks. In fact, a plumber had been called just a week ago and had made them as good as new. Saurabh Mathur pointed to the faucet above the sink and said, 'You should look at that one carefully. There's something very strange about it. We have repaired it thrice, but it starts dripping every time, always in the middle of the night.'

Sarbajeet positioned a motion sensor camera near that faucet.

The rest of the house was surveyed. Mr Mathur was in his room. He was asked to rest, but he was curious to see what was going on, so he continued to sit on a chair. Mrs Mathur was next to him, sitting silently and watching. The house consisted of two rooms, a hall, and a kitchen. A passageway connected these and led to the shared bathroom. There was another bathroom attached to the master bedroom, which was used by the old couple.

After the preliminary survey, Pooja came back with a puzzled look. 'It's difficult to say what we're up against this time,' she told Sarbajeet.

Sarbajeet walked around the house with the K2 meter, and when he came to the passageway facing the kitchen, things got rolling. There was a beep as the K2 meter lit up and blinked. He froze mid-step and Pooja rushed over to him. 'It's coming from in there,' Sarbajeet said, pointing to the kitchen.

Determining that there was indeed something there, he decided to initiate communication. He asked the Mathurs to stay in their rooms unless called, and then assuming his position by the doorway of the kitchen, he spoke out in a clear voice, 'Hello. I am Sarbajeet. Can you hear us?'

They expected no immediate answer.

Sarbajeet continued, 'We know you are here. Your behaviour has terrified this family. Come out and talk to us.'

Apart from the continued flashing of the K2 meter, there was no response.

It was about 2.30 in the afternoon. As it was a residential estate away from the roads, there was complete silence in the neighbourhood. The other families were asleep in their homes. The investigators had even closed all the windows of the Mathur house so that not even the muffled sounds of the television could be heard from the other houses.

It was in this silence that Sarbajeet warily took a step forward. Pooja wanted to say something as a precautionary measure, but she didn't. Sarbajeet asked the next question. 'I can sense you, you know? There's no point in hiding. Show yourself to us.'

That was a bold move. This entity was invisible and untested, but Sarbajeet decided to put up a brave front despite knowing all the havoc it had wreaked so far. 'I was filled with curiosity, for sure,' says Sarbajeet. 'If their accounts were correct, this was a kind of entity that we hadn't encountered before. I wanted to challenge it. In my mind, the entity was like a naughty child who needed to be reprimanded, and I had decided to be the strict teacher who would do that.'

Sarbajeet then stepped inside the kitchen. Pooja also followed him in. The kitchen was a large one, the kind typically found in old homes in the old residential buildings of Mumbai's suburbs. There was an L-shaped counter with the sink at its vertex. Sarbajeet also had his eye on that faucet. However, nothing worth mentioning was happening yet.

Then there was a noise. It was a short but sharp metallic clang. It came from the top shelves. There were several aluminium containers there, the kind used for storing flour and grain.

Sarbajeet pulled up a stool and climbed up. The shelf was wider than expected. There was space behind the boxes that could not be seen from below. The shelf itself was made of concrete and looked like part of the building's original design. Its ostensible purpose was to serve as an additional storage space. But situated on top like that, it was cut off from any light that the room received—the sun's rays coming in through the window during the day, and the light from the tube-light at night.

Very cautiously, Sarbajeet began to move the containers. He came to a corner behind the ledge. It was plunged in complete darkness. He switched on his mobile flashlight and shone it into the space. There was a big gap behind the shelf. The ceiling above was damp. Sarbajeet leant closer and was immediately assailed by a putrid smell of mould.

'There's something here,' Sarbajeet said. 'Some odd noise...'

'What do you hear?' Pooja asked.

Sarbajeet brought his ear closer to the loft. 'It's like a dull thud. Can you hear it?'

Pooja listened for it. There was absolute silence for a moment, and then it happened.

Thud-thud. It was the sound of one of those metal boxes being banged.

'There!' she said.

As if on cue, it happened again. *Thud-thud.*

'It's like it is mocking us,' said Pooja.

Sarbajeet decided to take a stern stand. In a harsher voice, he said, 'Stop playing games with us! Your antics aren't going to frighten us.'

This was followed by another spell of silence. But it was an ominous one. Sarbajeet had perhaps crossed a line by display of anger, but now there was no turning back.

And then they got what they were looking for. A loud, rattling sound came from somewhere close by. The sound was so loud and so sudden that Sarbajeet lost his balance and would have fallen off the stool. It pierced the silence of that afternoon. Sarbajeet hopped down and rushed out to see where it was coming from. Then it happened again. This time the source was clear. Saurabh also came out of his room and said, 'It's coming from the balcony.'

The three of them rushed to the balcony. And what they saw left them baffled.

There was an old iron rack in the balcony, which the Mathurs used for drying clothes. It was a standalone frame. The clotheslines were attached to it, and their other ends were tied to the hooks on the opposite wall. It was the iron rack that made all the noise. As they watched, it happened again. And this time, all three of them watched as the heavy iron frame wobbled on the floor as if the ground was vibrating.

They had hardly come out of the shock when they heard another noise, this time much louder—a heavy crash.

Mr Mathur came rushing out of his room. 'Look, look what's happened!' he yelled.

The three ran inside. What they saw left them speechless. His bookshelf had toppled over in his room, right in front of him. The most bizarre part was that the books were strewn all over the floor, and not just in the direction the bookshelf had collapsed.

'What's going on?' asked Mr Mathur. 'The bookshelf almost fell on me. I could have died.'

'It's all right, Mr Mathur,' Sarbajeet said. 'We are here to make sure that nothing happens.'

Sarbajeet ran up to the kitchen, which they knew was the source of all the mischief. He climbed back onto the stool and asked Pooja to hand him the thermometer. He aimed it at the spot right inside the loft and waited.

It confirmed many of their suspicions. The temperature of the place was 19 degrees Celsius, which was simply unbelievable, for the temperature outside at that time was 27 degrees Celsius.

'What could be causing so much havoc?' Pooja asked Sarbajeet. 'Never before have we encountered a spirit that could manifest itself so prominently. Moving that iron frame and bringing down the bookshelf—even a healthy living person would find that to be a bit of an effort.'

'It's a poltergeist,' said Sarbajeet.

'Oh, now I understand!' said Pooja. 'The noisy spirits.'

'Yes, exactly. They like to make their presence felt. That's why all the noise.' Sarbajeet turned to Saurabh. 'There's some good news and some bad news, brother. The good news is that it's not an evil spirit conjured up because of a hex that has been placed on your father. There is no curse on him. But the bad news is that this is a poltergeist.'

The colour drained from Saurabh's face. 'Does that mean you cannot remove it?'

'Poltergeists are extremely nasty and almost impossible to deal with,' Sarbajeet said. 'But we will try our best. This is a new challenge for us as well.'

'We need to come up with a plan to take it down,' said Pooja. 'Do you have anything in mind?'

Sarbajeet pondered. 'The thing with poltergeists is that they can gauge the abilities of humans in their presence. This one has understood that we have experience, so it's showing off a bit. That explains all the intense, noisy manifestations. The way we tackle this now would be to play its own game. If we can get the spirit to submit to us, we can probably tame it.'

'How do we do that?'

Sarbajeet stepped out into the corridor. He pointed to a tap and said, 'That's how.'

He was indicating the faucet.

It was a brilliant idea. Faucets were the favourite plaything of the poltergeists, as it turned out. It was like training a pet dog to do a new trick by making it do something familiar first.

Turning back to the kitchen, where the thuds had now intensified, Sarbajeet asked, 'Hi again. Let me introduce myself to you. I am Sarbajeet. You've already sensed my abilities, so I don't need to say any more. But what I cannot understand is what you are so angry about. We have seen what you did. Tell me, are these things your own doing or is someone else controlling you?'

A tense moment followed. No one spoke, but the family and the investigators were now looking up at the loft in the kitchen. The dull thudding noise was still there. If anything, it had slightly increased in volume. It had a clear double beat and sounded like a heartbeat.

Thud-thud...thud-thud...thud-thud...

'I can sense that it is just a single entity,' said Pooja.

Sarbajeet nodded. 'Come on, now,' he said. 'Show me something else. Can you do something I say? Can you perhaps turn on the faucet for me? These people tell me you love doing that.'

Nothing happened, apart from the relentless thudding.

'Won't you do it?' Sarbajeet urged. 'Look at these faucets. I'm sure you can do it. Come on. I bet you cannot turn them on.'

He stepped towards the faucet in the sink—the one where the motion sensor camera was positioned. All five pairs of eyes were now fixed on the faucet.

'You can't, right?' Sarbajeet said, without taking his eyes off the faucet.

And then the light from the motion sensor camera switched on.

The old Mathurs held each other in shock. Saurabh stepped back. They had been anticipating it, but seeing it happen in front of their eyes was unnerving. A faint trickle of water had started from the faucet! It was only a few drops, but there was no reason why that should happen with a faucet that had just been fixed.

'Oh my God!' said Mrs Mathur. 'You made him do it.'

And then everyone flinched. There was another loud sound, this time from the kitchen. The group ran to see that the kitchen sink tap was turned on in all its glory.

The poltergeist turned to be extremely difficult to drive out from the house. It was definitely a poltergeist and not a product of black magic or voodoo. The poltergeist must have made its abode in the kitchen loft, which was not surprising, for these entities seek out such nooks and crannies in inhabited houses that are mostly inaccessible to humans. Poltergeists are known to love human company!

It took them three days to remove the poltergeist. Sarbajeet and Pooja requested the family to move into their daughter Varsha's house. With the house empty, the poltergeist was challenged several times by Sarbajeet, each time weakening its resolve. The entire investigation was bizarre. The first day was punctuated by a string of unnatural occurrences, including sounds of crashing and banging and things falling over unexpectedly and dangerously. Other team members were called in from the second day. On the second day, it seemed that the poltergeist was becoming weaker. The ploy of constantly challenging it seemed to be working. By the third day, they sensed that the spirit had reached a manageable level of vulnerability. At an appropriate time, an elaborate cleansing ritual was performed with salt water poured copiously into all corners of the old house, especially the loft. They then burned Californian sage, and the fumes were aired throughout the house for almost 30 minutes.

The deed was done and confirmed when Pooja sensed the original aura of the house return. 'The negativity of the house receded and it became bright and clear, like someone with a long-standing vision problem finally gets a pair of spectacles and begins to see everything clearly,' says Pooja.

And thus, one of the most bizarre projects in the history of PAIRS came to an end.

Poltergeist

Poltergeists are among the oldest entities known to us. Their chief trait is that they are highly elusive and are rarely spotted. The name has a German origin—*polter* means 'to make a sound', and *geist* means 'ghost'. Thus, poltergeist literally means 'a noisy ghost'. In all historical and current accounts of poltergeists, this is seen to be true. These entities are infamous for being able to physically manipulate their environment. They can produce sounds such as those of crashing, thudding, hammering, clanging and many others that we would describe as noise, and often these noises are quite audible and annoying. Some of the more powerful ones are also capable of throwing objects across rooms, knocking over furniture and even tripping people.

Paranormal investigators believe that poltergeists are highly intelligent beings. They can learn to use new technology in their environment, which is usually within human dwellings. When the age of electricity began, poltergeists learnt to play with appliances. They played with switches, making motor-based appliances such as washing machines, mixer-grinders, electric fans move, dimming or brightening electric lights, turning television sets on or off—these were the activities they indulged in. The more recent poltergeists are also known to manipulate electronic devices such as laptops and mobile phones.

Among ghostly entities, poltergeists might very well be the oldest type of spirits mentioned. One of the earliest mentions of poltergeist activity can be found in the account of the Jewish historian Flavius Josephus, who was born in Jerusalem and later lived in Rome. He is known for his accounts of the Jewish-Roman wars that were fought in his time. Among his numerous reports, he also describes an exorcism in detail. This account dates back to AD 94. Josephus was witness to an exorcism performed by a man named Eleazar. The victim was a man whom the possessing spirit had turned unclean. The exorcism was successful, but something remarkable happened at the exact moment the spirit left the man's body. When Eleazar pronounced that the spirit was leaving the body, a bowl of water that was at the other end of the room very noisily upturned by itself. There was no one near the bowl at the time. Eleazar declared that the spirit, in its malevolent anger at being driven away from its host, had vengefully upturned that bowl of water.

This is considered by many to be the first poltergeist account, though in the days that it occurred there was no special classification such as 'poltergeist'.

The case of the Bell Witch is known to almost everyone with a penchant for dark and mysterious phenomena. This incident took place in Tennessee over several years in the early nineteenth century. It also attracted a great deal of

Hollywood attention, and many films were made about the Bell Witch. The subject of these hauntings was a man named John Bell. His family lived on a farm.

One day, all of a sudden, several unnatural occurrences began to take place. Abnormal noises came from the walls, the furniture was moved, things were thrown around the house, and even people were reportedly slapped by invisible forces. The animals on the farm were also spooked and began to leave one by one. One particularly hair-raising incident was when a monstrous creature (a hybrid between a dog and a rabbit) suddenly appeared on the farm. These events also destabilized their family life. Betsy Bell, John Bell's daughter, lost her suitor. An investigator who came to check on the house was almost killed when the wheels of his carriage suddenly stopped and the horses bolted.

But, just as mysteriously as the Bell Witch occurrences began, they ended in a similar fashion. People ended up speculating about who the culprit was. The most popular theory was that it was the spirit of Kate Batts, a woman whom John Bell had taken advantage of, and then killed. During her lifetime, this woman was said to have dabbled in the dark arts. It was believed that her spirit had returned to haunt the Bells.

The chilling account of the Bell Witch is a clear indication of poltergeist activity because of the sheer physical nature of these hauntings.

Explanation and Criticism

Since poltergeist activities have been so clearly witnessed and recorded by people all around the world, there have been many attempts to understand why it happens. Who are poltergeists, and where do they come from?

According to paranormal experts, *poltergeists are intelligent spirits which are able to manipulate their physical surroundings in the living world.* They are considered the lowest class of spirits and are regarded as mischief-mongers. Poltergeists like to stay close to human habitations, such as people's homes, and hidden and dark places therein. This makes them different from other kinds of ghosts who shy away from human inhabitation and localize themselves in desolate and abandoned places.

How and when a poltergeist makes its abode in a human residence is unknown. But when a poltergeist appears, it makes its presence felt almost immediately. It begins with soft sounds that cannot be explained. After a short time, these turn into more clear manifestations, such as the moving and toppling of furniture. True to their name, poltergeists engage in quite noisy activities, and the occupants of the house can tell that something has happened the moment it takes place.

No one has ever seen a poltergeist or its physical form. This is unlike ectoplasmic ghosts who sometimes may appear in the form of fog, mist, shadows or something similar. Poltergeists are either very good at keeping themselves hidden, or have no physical form whatsoever. Perhaps this is the reason why they are able to focus all their energies on creating noisy disturbances in the living world. Though a poltergeist itself can never be seen, its activities can be very clearly perceived.

Most poltergeists are not believed to be vicious or evil. Though there have been instances when people have reported being slapped or tripped, it does not usually go beyond that. It is believed that despite all their naughtiness, poltergeists do not intend to harm the humans they live with.

It is understandable that poltergeists, like all other paranormal phenomena, have elicited their fair share of scepticism. There have been many theories attempting to debunk activities that have been attributed to poltergeists.

One of these theories, which we shall call the Old House Theory, takes off on the fact that most reported poltergeist activities occur in old houses. Age leads to weathering. Plumbing lines, in particular, can cause vibrations in houses as they age. As water flows through them, the vibrations can become audible in the form of rumbling noises, and in some cases, they can also move objects placed directly above or near the pipes. These could also cause fixtures like faucets to behave erratically, and cause seepage on walls, both of which are commonly reported occurrences by people claiming poltergeist activity.

According to critics, old furniture could also be the culprit for many of these 'poltergeist' sounds. Furniture, especially those made of hardwood, weathers over time. They begin to develop internal cracks, which can produce strange noises. Furniture is also known to expand and contract during the day due to temperature conditions. In the daytime, these sounds are not audible, but at night they are clear in the absence of most other sounds.

Sometimes, the cause of paranormal activity might be found in the psyche of the person who is subjected to it. Some hallucinations can be extremely intense, and when coupled with auditory hallucinations, can make the person believe that things are happening around them that are actually not happening. Psychoanalysts also point to wishful thinking, a psychological behaviour where a person wants to believe in something so strongly that they begin to actually see it. In a more direct explanation, a poltergeist activity might be caused by a memory lapse. One might forget an action carried out by them, such as leaving a book on a table, and then think that this has been done by a paranormal force.

There is also a strong criticism that many of these so-called paranormal activities could be outright hoaxes or pranks. But if they are, they can just as easily be discovered as such. As Sarbajeet says, 'Hoaxes do happen. But if even one in a hundred cases is genuine, we need to get to the bottom of it, because poltergeists can be very nasty and detrimental to the family they reside with.'

In another case in Pune, Sarbajeet had a brush with a poltergeist which bolstered his belief in the existence of these entities.

Again, this was an old house occupied only by an old caretaker and a black Alsatian dog. The house had recently been purchased by a family which still had not moved in. This family had heard certain things about the house from the neighbours. One of the neighbours told them that strange noises could be heard from the house throughout the night. The old caretaker was partially deaf and thus could not hear it. The dog, however, howled at odd hours during the night. The neighbours were certain that there was something in the house that needed to be taken care of.

The family, who had already purchased the house, were distraught. They decided to have the house investigated by a paranormal investigation team before moving in, and that was where PAIRS came in.

An investigation was duly scheduled. The caretaker and the dog were still in the house, as the new family had allowed them to stay on. Sarbajeet and his team visited the house, and after the initial surveillance, asked the caretaker to lock himself up in a room with the dog, since they did not know what they were dealing with.

The investigation followed the usual course. Soon activity was reported on the devices. The presence of something was soon established. Pooja could sense that it was a tiny-sized spirit, probably that of a child who had been living in the location, if not in the house itself, for ages. She also perceived that the spirit was angry about something and adamant that the property was his. It was this territorial authority that had made the spirit obstinate.

Soon this turned out to be a very noisy investigation. At one point, a door was slammed in a team member's face. The team member narrowly escaped a severe injury. Pooja felt her legs being dragged. Had she not been wary that something like this could happen, she would have a bad fall.

The poltergeist activity was detected in the middle of the night, when the investigation was at its zenith. While Sarbajeet was trying to pinpoint the exact location the spirit had occupied in the house, there was a loud crashing sound. The sound was louder than something crashing on the floor; it sounded like someone had dashed a wooden object onto the floor with all their might. And there was another odd thing about it—the crash ended with a series of twangs which produced a bizarre musical note.

Sarbajeet and his team spread out around the house to see where the sound was coming from. The old caretaker had also opened the door. The noise was so loud that even he could hear it despite his poor hearing. The dog was still tied to a bed-post because, as the caretaker said, he was not too friendly to guests.

The investigation resumed. Sarbajeet went back to finding out the source of the activity: the hub from where it all started. His devices were proving unreliable, as they were responding to almost everywhere in the house.

Unable to find the spot from where the negativity was emanating, Sarbajeet decided to do a generic cleansing of the house and leave. Given the kind of activity that they had seen in the house, this was not a very effective solution, but there was no other way. A saltwater cleansing of all the areas of the house was duly performed. That accomplished, the team prepared to leave.

They were almost at the door when the dog suddenly became restless. Still tied to his leash, he began to pace around the room, breathing heavily. Sarbajeet observed the animal's odd behaviour and stopped. It was then that the dog began to bark furiously. It was 1.30 a.m. and the team was worried that the barking might wake the neighbours, but nothing they did could placate the animal.

Then Sarbajeet observed that the dog was barking in one particular direction. He was looking at a particular wall of the room and barking. Sarbajeet inspected the wall. There was nothing of note there. However, as the barking continued, Sarbajeet walked around the wall, came out of the door, and saw the other room of the house. The team had already been in this room during the early hours of the investigation, and had inspected it thoroughly.

They opened the room again. It was dark inside, and when the team switched on the lights, they were aghast to find a guitar on the floor. The instrument was completely smashed and the strings had come loose. They realized that this was the source of the crashing noise which had culminated in a musical note.

Once again, Sarbajeet resumed his investigation. There was a large metal cabinet in the room. According to the caretaker, the guitar had been placed on top of it. The team then moved the heavy cupboard, and were shocked to find that the wall behind it had completely rotted away due to water leakage. A large gaping hole in the wall stared at them.

Further investigation revealed that this was the home of the spirit, which was, in fact, a poltergeist. A full cleansing ritual was carried out and a follow-up investigation a month later showed that the supernatural activity in the house had ceased.

I have mentioned the cases here where Sarbajeet and his team actually had genuine encounters with poltergeists. Sarbajeet admits that they receive dozens of calls regarding apparent poltergeist activity, but most of them turn out to be false alarms. Real poltergeist activity, when it occurs, is quite terrifying. For a majority of the reported incidents, however, there are entirely plausible explanations that have nothing to do with the paranormal.

SHOWING THEM THE WAY HOME

Exorcism

'Is the human body a vessel for spirits? What happens if someone takes over it? Where does the spirit go?'

—Eli Roth

Late one evening in 2018, Sarbajeet's doorbell rang frantically. It was after 11 and the young paranormal investigator was planning to retire for the day. With some curiosity, he opened the door. It was his neighbour Ajit standing outside the door with a terrified expression on his face. His messy hair and the sweat on his forehead accentuated that expression.

'Sarbajeet, bro, I need your help urgently,' he said.

Sarbajeet was shaken by his voice and appearance. 'What happened? Tell me.'

In halting words, Ajit told him that something bizarre was going on with his wife Sushma. Ever since she had returned from her mother's house two days ago, she had been behaving oddly. 'She refuses to eat and doesn't leave the bed at all,' Ajit said. 'At first I thought it was exhaustion from the trip. But now she has started making low growling sounds and doing weird stuff like biting her nails and scratching the paint off the walls. She also pulls her hair out. Our daughter Isha went into the room in the evening to check on her and found her in a peculiar position on the bed—she was half on the bed and half on the floor; her head was dangling off the bed, and she was singing something. Isha called me in panic. The next moment, Sushma sprang up from the bed and lunged at Isha's throat. My poor child is shaken! Who attacks their own daughter like that? Since then, she has not come out of her room. We are even scared to open her door. She thumps on the furniture and jumps on the bed and beats the walls. She has become uncontrollable, Sarbajeet. I don't know...do you think she's possessed?'

'Relax, relax!' Sarbajeet said. 'One must not jump to conclusions. You said this started two days ago. Did you go to the doctor?'

'No, I did not get the chance. But if you take a look at her, you will understand that this is not a usual medical issue. Please come with me, Sarbajeet. Aren't you an exorcist?'

Sarbajeet gave it some thought. 'See, I will come but let me tell you a few things beforehand. Possessions are very rare. Most of the time, it's something else entirely. And you say you haven't even taken her to a doctor yet. You need to rule out all medical causes first.'

'But Sarbajeet...where will I go at this hour? You please look at her. Just talk to her. You can do that, can't you?'

'Yes, I can. You are a neighbour and a friend, so I can do this for you. But don't expect too much, all right?'

With this warning, the two men walked up the few

flights of stairs to Ajit's house. His daughter Isha opened the door. She had a grim expression on her face.

Sarbajeet stepped inside. Almost immediately, his ear was assailed by a loud bang coming from one of the rooms. 'She is in there,' Ajit said.

'Can you open the door?' Sarbajeet asked. 'I will try to talk to her.'

Very cautiously, Ajit proceeded towards the door. He said in a gentle voice, 'Sushma, my dear, someone is here to meet you. He's our friend. He wants to talk to you. I am opening the door, okay?'

The room fell into complete silence at these words. Ajit kept his hand on the doorknob and, after casting one look at Sarbajeet, he opened the door. Then he quickly stepped aside as if he were afraid to face the person inside.

Sarbajeet pushed the door all the way open. But no sooner had he taken a step into the room than the woman shrieked as if all hell had broken loose. 'Get out of here! Get out! I don't want to see your face. I don't want to talk to you!'

Those baleful words were uttered in such a high-pitched voice that Sarbajeet immediately backed away. The woman ran to the door and locked it again. She shouted from inside, once again in the same hellish voice, 'Take him away! Take him away! I don't want to meet anyone! If you bring anyone with you, I will kill this woman.'

Ajit sharply turned at Sarbajeet. 'Did you hear that? *I will kill this woman.* She is referring to herself in the third person. There is something else in her now. She is possessed.'

Sarbajeet sat down on a chair. He contemplated his

course of action. Something occurred to him, and he said, 'Ajit, I need to talk to your wife. Only then can we find the truth. You tell your wife that I have gone home. When you open the door, you and your daughter will hold her. I will then ask her a few questions.'

Ajit's eyes twinkled at this suggestion. Sarbajeet was willing to help him. He was still wary of going near his wife, but he understood what he had to do.

The ruse worked. Ajit told Sushma that Sarbajeet had left and a few minutes later she opened the door. Ajit asked her to lie down on the bed to rest and then he held her by the arms. The moment Sarbajeet walked in, the woman started violently thrashing and flailing her arms and legs, but her husband and daughter tried their best to hold her down. It was a difficult task for the two of them, as accompanying the physical struggle was the emotional trauma of hearing the worst obscenities that were now freely flowing out of the woman's mouth. They were most terrible expletives, and Ajit was shocked that his wife even knew those words, let alone utter them.

I saw a different side of Sarbajeet when he described this scene to me. Normally a calm, level-headed person, Sarbajeet's mind seemed to be beset with some agitation. When I asked, he said, 'Neil brother, I was really shaken by what I saw. I had been to Ajit's house before and Sushma bhabhi had always been so hospitable and soft-spoken. She made you feel at ease, you know? Her aura was so comforting…and she doted on her daughter. And now to see her in this state mouthing all those terrible words of abuse; it was a complete shocker.'

'I want to know what happened next,' I said.

Sarbajeet returned to his narration:

In a solemn but stern voice, Sarbajeet began the conversation, 'Hi, Sushma…'

The woman's eyes immediately flickered open. 'I am not Sushma!' she said in a throaty voice, a strand of spittle flowing from the corner of her mouth.

'Okay, you are not Sushma. Then who are you?'

'I am Lakshmi, you dog!'

Sarbajeet did not flinch at this direct abuse. He went a step further and said, 'All right, Lakshmi. I don't want you to be afraid of me. I am not here to hurt you.'

The woman laughed. As she laughed, Sarbajeet could see her yellowed and stinking teeth, which, as Ajit had mentioned, she hadn't brushed since returning from her mother's place. In fact, she hadn't even changed her clothes. 'You can't hurt me, you rat!' she cackled.

The woman did not answer his question. Sarbajeet extended his arm at her. But just as he was about to place his hand on her forehead, the woman's body sharply lurched in the air, and she tried to clamp Sarbajeet's wrist in her mouth. Sarbajeet, who had been extremely cautious, withdrew his hand just in time, or she would have bitten off a piece of his arm.

'She has no fever,' Sarbajeet told Ajit. Then he asked her further, 'Lakshmi, tell me why you are here. What do you want?'

The woman continued to stare at Sarbajeet, obviously disappointed that she was unable to take a bite. In a low, growling voice, she said, 'I hate this bitch. I am going to kill this bitch.'

Ajit almost cried. 'What has she done?' he asked.

Then the woman snapped again. Looking at his face with the utmost spite, she said, 'You stay out of this, you pig-f*cker.'

Sarbajeet continued, 'You're just talking to me, Lakshmi. I can understand you. You tell me. Why do you want to hurt Sushma?'

Then something very curious happened. The woman did not answer this question, but she narrowed her eyes, and her eyelids began to flutter, just like you see in movies when someone goes into a trance. This was accompanied by a weird grin on her face, which looked both like a smile and a pained expression. Then she made a continuous clicking sound with her tongue that sounded like '*Ki ki ki ki ki ki*...'

Isha was trembling by now. Tears flowed down her face profusely. Amid her crying, she said, 'Mumma...what has happened to you?'

The woman's hand instantly lashed out. It was with much greater energy than she had shown before. The hand was aimed directly at Isha's face, and it hit her hard. The girl was about 10 years old and well built, but the impact of that slap made her reel backwards, and crash on the ground with a bleeding lip.

Sarbajeet grabbed hold of the woman just before she could dash and hit someone else. Ajit helped him while he kept an eye on Isha to see if she was hurt. The struggle continued for another minute and then, all of a sudden, it died down.

The woman went limp and sat on the bed.

The moaning and clacking, the wide-eyed stares, the twitching of the lips, all ceased. What made the difference, probably, was that Isha was now bleeding from the lip. The mother in Sushma could not bear the sight of her daughter's blood. 'Oh no…she hit Isha…she hit Isha…' she kept repeating.

Sarbajeet noticed this difference. He gently asked, 'Hi, are you Sushma?'

This time, she nodded.

Ajit was overjoyed, but Sarbajeet held him back. 'Sushma, are you all right?' he asked.

Sushma shook her head.

'Why? What is wrong?'

'She is inside me,' Sushma said. 'She is a very bad woman.'

Sarbajeet, now strengthened by this dramatic change of scene, said, 'Sushma, you are safe with me. Will you tell me exactly what happened?'

Then Sushma began. Her voice was broken and she spoke so softly that one had to strain to hear, as if she was trying to withhold her words from forming fully. 'On the last day of my visit to my mother's house, I went to the riverbank. I usually visit the river when I go to my hometown. There was no one with me. As the sun was about to set, I turned back homeward. But I saw something that made me stop. About 200 metres away from where I was standing, something was burning on the riverbank. It was a funeral pyre. The family and a pandit were standing next to the fire. I went to see if it was someone I knew. My mother's village is small, and we all know each other.'

Sarbajeet assured her that he was listening. 'Go on, Sushma.'

'I stood near the burning pyre. Then I saw the face of the person who had died. It was a woman about my age. Someone mentioned her name—Lakshmi. She had come to the village about 10 years ago after her marriage. She had no child. She had died of an illness. People were talking about her sad life. A man there who knew me pointed out that Lakshmi and I were married in the same year, but I had a happy life in Mumbai, whereas Lakshmi had lived such a sad life. He did not say that in spite, just to remind me of my blessings and to be grateful. I was sad, and turned to leave.'

'What happened then?'

'Just as I turned around, there was a loud bang behind me. I don't know what the noise was, but it came from the pyre. Nobody else seemed to have heard it. But I did, and the next moment I saw something rising from the smoke. The whole world began to turn around me. I suddenly felt suffocated and in someone's grip. I cannot explain it. And then I blanked out.'

'And then?'

'When I came to my senses, I was here. Then I felt that I was not alone. Lakshmi had come with me. She is here now. She is right here and she is...oh my God... she is very angry.'

Sushma fell silent again. Her head suddenly drooped as if she had lost all voluntary control over it and her hair, which was already in disarray, fell to either side of her face, hiding it completely.

'Sushma, are you all right?' Sarbajeet asked.

Then a chillingly calm voice slowly rang out again, 'Sushma doesn't want to talk to you anymore.'

Sarbajeet asked Ajit and Isha to go out of the room. He also followed them and locked the room from outside. They sat in silence for a few moments. Then Sarbajeet spoke, 'I think I know what's wrong with your wife, Ajit.'

'What is it?'

'There is good news and bad news.'

'Bad news first.'

'The bad news is that your wife cannot be exorcised.'

'Cannot be exorcised? But aren't you a certified exorcist?'

'That I am, but it still cannot be done.'

'Why?'

'Now I'll come to the good news. It is because your wife is not possessed at all!'

Ajit brightened up. 'No, she isn't?'

'Rest assured; she isn't. Let me explain. Sushma went to her hometown. She saw the cremation. When she saw the face of the dead woman, who was her age, it unnerved her. Then people started comparing them. It played on her psyche. Also consider the atmosphere. It was evening, it was getting dark, a lonely riverbank, and a cremation. That can play with anyone's mind. Somewhere along the way, she developed this split personality and thought she was Lakshmi. And Lakshmi is angry with Sushma because they both come from the same village and yet Sushma has such a better life than her. Your wife's own guilt has arisen because of the comparison. You have seen that there are absolutely no physical symptoms.'

The words made Ajit happy. For a moment the smile lingered on his lips, then a frown appeared again. 'But what about the bang? That blanking out?'

Sarbajeet leant forward. 'Have you ever stayed a cremation till the very end?'

Ajit shook his head.

'Isha, you may not want to hear this,' Sarbajeet told Isha, who obliged and went to another room. Then he continued, 'When a corpse is burnt, the flesh burns first and then the bones. You can hear the cracking of the bones as the fire spreads to them. But when it reaches the skull, the brain inside melts away first. This creates a hollow space inside the skull. An enormous amount of smoke builds up in there, so much that it often causes the skull to crack open. The noise is so loud that it sounds like a bomb exploding.'

'Oh my God! But she says she was the only one to hear it.'

'I am sure everyone else heard it too. But they were the mourning family. Or maybe they knew the sound was coming and were expecting it. They were all men evidently, so they must have known the sound. It's actually quite a routine thing at cremations, really.

'So that was what must have triggered the whole thing? And the black thing she saw was the smoke,' Ajit mused. 'It all makes sense now. But what do we do with her now?'

'Now you know there's nothing unnatural about her,' said Sarbajeet. 'You need to talk to her about it and tell her that there's nothing to worry about. Lakshmi is only in her mind and since it is a very recent memory, a little bit of love and understanding will take care of it. And do visit a doctor tomorrow morning.'

Ajit did as he was told. Within just a week or so,

Sushma's aggressiveness dwindled, though it would be a whole year before she returned to normalcy. The family came to meet Sarbajeet later, but Sushma had very little recollection of what had transpired during those two bizarre nights.

Exorcism

Sarbajeet Mohanty, a certified demonologist, is one of the few people in the world authorized to perform exorcisms. He is often approached by people who believe that their friends or family members are possessed by something. However, Sarbajeet goes right out to say that there are many myths surrounding the subject, including the fact that only a miniscule fraction of all exorcism cases involve possession by paranormal entities.

Exorcism is not merely what has become popular in horror literature and movies. There are several other sides to it. The paranormal world describes exorcism as follows.

An exorcism is the cleansing of the energy in a person's aura or space, which may or may not involve a paranormal entity.

This definition has two parts that are worth mentioning.

The first aspect of exorcism, 'cleansing', specifies exactly what it is. Paranormal experts believe in the concept of auras around living beings, which are energy fields that surround each one of us. Auras are unique to every individual and also change according to our emotional state. Negative auras have a negative effect on us; they can plunge us into a state of grief, despair, lack of confidence, or fear, and in extreme cases they can cause long-standing mental health issues such as depression and even suicidal thoughts.

In Sarbajeet's experience, most cases that were believed to be possessions were in fact nothing but instances of negative energy. These had either accumulated in the person over a period of time or were triggered by a sudden incident. In such cases, 'to exorcise the person' actually means getting rid of the negative energies and putting the person in a positive frame of mind.

The second aspect of exorcism as mentioned in the definition is that the process 'may or may not pertain to a paranormal entity.' Although the existence of ethereal entities cannot be totally discounted, most cases of exorcism do not deal with them. In many situations, exorcism is a 'correction' of energies in the surroundings of the affected person. This can include the room, the house, the immediate exteriors, and even personal possessions. Certain objects and experiences can affect us adversely. Sometimes, exorcism might just mean investigating the root cause of the issue, identifying the object or experience that triggered it, and then trying to obliterate it from the person's psyche.

The Process of Exorcism

Sarbajeet notes that the manner in which exorcisms are portrayed in films is not entirely correct. Films tend to have a certain degree of fabrication and dramatization. The process of exorcism, as he conducts it, involves the following stages:

1. Examining the person's aura and ruling out medical causes
2. Understanding the person by interviewing people close to them
3. Identifying the triggering event or emotional situation underlying the cause
4. Attempting to bring the person to a normal state by resolving the issue
5. A systematic spiritual cleansing of the person and their environment

While sharing details of his methodology, Sarbajeet warns readers that a true exorcism can be a very dangerous procedure, especially when a paranormal entity is involved, and that it should never be performed by someone who hasn't extensively studied it.

There is another grim warning that Sarbajeet issues when he speaks on the subject of exorcism. Exorcism is grossly misunderstood in India, especially in smaller, rural towns where the practice is carried out by self-proclaimed godmen of dubious reputation. Often these are deviant practices associated with black magic. There are horrific claims that women, in particular, are possessed and alleged exorcisms are performed on them in full view of the public. People who claim to perform these exorcisms generally end up harming the women irrevocably, even to the extent of brutalizing them with rape. These are ghastly stories that are, sadly, a reality even in the present day in certain parts of the country. Sarbajeet vehemently refuses to accept these vile practices as true forms of exorcism, and states that this is just another way for patriarchy to establish its dominance over women and that such practices must be rooted out of our tradition.

A genuine exorcism is rarely about chasing out spirits or demons, although this cannot be discounted. In the rare case that an otherworldly entity is involved, an elaborate procedure must be performed to expel the presence from the person, and this can only come by gaining the right kind of knowledge and expertise. Of all the cases of exorcism that Sarbajeet has shared with me, I will describe one case where he encountered the presence of a paranormal entity in the person.

Arun was a young man living in Pune. In addition to a regular job, he ran a successful travel blog for which he travelled around the world. In the course of his country-hopping, this intrepid young fellow would always bring back some kind of small memento from the countries he visited. His fridge door was peopled with magnets from all over the world, and the many display cabinets in his hall were overflowing with curios such as pens, dolls, trinkets, showpieces and other such objects.

Weird things started happening shortly after a particular curio came into his possession. It was an ivory man curio. While he was still travelling, he had nightmares in hotel rooms. His extensive travelling experiences had opened his mind up to bizarre events. He believed that these nightmares, in which he usually saw hooded figures and serpents, were caused by sheer psychological exhaustion, odd magnetic fields in the regions, or the position of his hotel bed in the wrong direction.

A few days later, he returned home where the series of unusual phenomena continued. He had a dog Marcus—a hefty Doberman—who usually rushed to him whenever he returned home from those long trips. However, on this occasion, Marcus did not run up to him. In fact, the moment Arun entered the house, Marcus whimpered like a brow-beaten puppy and cowered in a corner with his tail tucked between his legs. Arun still did not give it a lot of importance; he thought that perhaps it was his appearance—he was wearing a black scarf with a skull pattern purchased in the Netherlands—that had frightened the dog.

That night, he had a lucid dream, in which he saw scenes of his escapades in Europe and—the most curious thing of all—his dream ended with the ivory man curio. His sleep was interrupted. He got that thing out of his bag and examined it. There was nothing odd about it at all—it was hardly the length of a finger. He kept the innocuous thing on his desk.

Later that night, Marcus began barking his head off. Arun and his mother, who lived in the house, tried their best to comfort the dog, but to no avail. The next day, the dog started behaving even more peculiarly. He followed Arun cautiously, making sure to stay well behind him, and barked at the slightest provocation.

This did not stay restricted in the house. Over the next few days after that, Arun occasionally had the feeling that someone was sitting in the back seat of his car. He would turn to look in shock, once even dangerously losing control of his car, but there was no one there. He also had this feeling on multiple instances in his office. Electric lights would behave erratically, windowpanes would vibrate on their own, things would fall off his desk on their own, and his computer would flicker. Then, one evening, just as he had turned away from the coffeemaker after filling his cup, there was an explosion. He was horror-struck to see that the coffeemaker had exploded. There was no apparent reason why this might have happened.

That was when he decided to approach Sarbajeet. Arun was open to the idea of ghosts and spirits. He told Sarbajeet upfront that there was a presence of an entity in his house that he had probably picked up on his travels. On the way to his house, Sarbajeet asked him as many questions as possible. Sarbajeet paid particular attention when he talked about the souvenirs he had brought home.

Once at his house, Sarbajeet asked Arun to go into the bedroom with his mother and Marcus, and lock themselves in. He was going to embark on a thorough investigation of the house, and it was best if they stayed out of the way. Before they entered the bedroom, Sarbajeet explored it thoroughly with the K2 meter. There was nothing in there that was out of the ordinary. Once the family was out of the way, Sarbajeet scanned each and every corner of the house. He spent a good hour investigating every nook and cranny but came up with nothing.

Sarbajeet thought of concluding that there was nothing out of place in the house. He kept his equipment on the table and called Arun out so that he could have a chat with him. Sarbajeet sat down on a chair next to the table while Arun paced around the room, still in a highly excited state. Sarbajeet told him that he had not found any presence and perhaps all that was happening was just a coincidence.

At that point, Arun came to sit on the chair next to the Sarbajeet. Then something strange happened. No sooner did Arun come within the range of the K2 meter than it lit up as if it were a shop sign during peak hours! Sarbajeet was immediately alarmed and asked Arun to step back and come closer once again. He did that. The device stopped lighting up as he moved away, and lit up again as he approached. Sarbajeet realized with great shock that whatever the entity was, it had now latched on to Arun.

Sarbajeet asked Arun to sit down. He now had a bigger question on his mind. That there was an entity inside Arun was established. But was this entity a simple spirit, or a demon? Demons are known to possess humans, and travellers occasionally pick them up in far-flung destinations of the world. To test whether it was a demon, Sarbajeet at first started subtly using the names of various gods in his conversations. Each time he uttered the name of a god, he looked intently into Arun's eyes for any reaction. Demons always react to the names of gods who are their nemeses. But nothing seemed to change in Arun. There was another test to be conducted to confirm this. Sarbajeet carried a bottle of holy water in his bag (not the religious holy water, but water energized with herbs and salt that he uses), and without warning, he sprinkled a few drops of the water on Arun. Sarbajeet knew it wouldn't be like in the movies—there would be no immediate burning of the skin or anything like that—but a demonic presence would still recoil when touched by holy water. Nothing of the sort happened.

Sarbajeet was certain that he wasn't dealing with a demon. The entity inside Arun was an ordinary ghost of a human he had picked up. That was when he remembered the mementos that Arun collected. Upon asking, Arun remembered the lucid dream he had. He said that the figurine had appeared in his dream shortly after his return. Sarbajeet put two and two together. It was highly likely that this figurine had been the ghost's vessel for a long time, and it had now passed on to Arun. Now it had to be flushed out of Arun and transferred back into the object.

Sarbajeet asked Arun for the figurine. But try as he might, he could not find it in the house. He searched for a long time in all the cupboards and drawers and everywhere he could have kept it. The figurine was nowhere to be found. Sarbajeet reiterated the need to find it, because after the exorcism, the entity would want to go back into its original abode.

Then Arun's mother suddenly recalled where it was. She opened her box of sewing threads and took the figurine out. She said that she had felt something suffocating about that object and, because of that bad feeling, she had stuffed it inside the box, and then forgotten about it.

That was it then. Sarbajeet placed the figurine next to Arun, and conducted an elaborate exorcism. He performed an hour-long rite, and frequently sprinkled salt-water on Arun, and rubbed his body with sage leaves. A few long minutes later, Arun let out a loud sigh. Sarbajeet quickly placed the figurine in a little black bag and tied it up with a black satin thread. Arun was now exorcised.

Arun felt better in a matter of days. The darkness in his mind had vanished, and he was ready to travel again, although he would now be careful what souvenirs he brought back home.

As for the figurine itself, Sarbajeet knew it was dangerous to keep it. He buried the object deep in the ground in a desolate jungle area. He had to keep the object away from human habitations because he had perceived that the spirit inside it was eager to latch on to the next human that would come its way.

I asked Sarbajeet to take me to the location and show me the ivory man, but he vehemently refused. 'Neil brother,' he said, 'you write horror and deal with the paranormal every day, even if indirectly. You are almost a psychic. It's best you stay away from such elements of darkness, or I'll have another case on my hands.'

I will remember Sarbajeet's solemn face as he said that for as long as I live.

~

In paranormal courses, there are case studies of exorcisms which are part of the syllabus. For his ordainment, Sarbajeet was assigned a particular case—that of a girl from England in the 1800s. The girl was brought to the church as she exhibited terrifying, inhuman symptoms that left no doubt that there was something completely unnatural about her. The priests concluded that her body was a vessel for demons, and they were many in number. An exorcism rite was performed in full view of the attending parsons, and it turned out to be the most harrowing experience of her life. As the priests performed the rite, the demons started getting released from the girl's body. But so powerful were these demons that each time one was exorcised from the girl's body, it would be ejected from her violently, leaving a terrible injury on the girl's body in their wake. Those present watched in horror as her bones cracked and skin ripped apart as each demon left her. The rite was completed days later, and the priest who captained the exorcism put it on record that the girl had 1,400 demons inside her.

However, despite its popularity as a topic in parapsychology, exorcism is a much-misunderstood topic. Even the books and films about it have done it quite a disservice. When performed properly, exorcism is a healing rite that can vastly improve the quality of life of a person surrounded by negative energies—both natural and paranormal.

THE MONSTERS OF SLEEP

Sleep Paralysis

'I wake up in the middle of the night and I can't move.'

—Kendall Jenner

Naved came to PAIRS with an extraordinary request. He was a young entrepreneur of 27, well-educated from a convent school of Mumbai. He grabbed the attention of the team right from his first, very intriguing statement. This is what he said, quite simply, 'Guys, I think I am haunted by a demon.'

Sarbajeet's interest was immediately piqued, as he had researched both Indian and Western demonology. He asked, 'What kind of demon? Give us the specifics.'

Naved began his explanation. 'I have a retail shop that sells mobile phones. My house is near my shop. I work in two shifts, morning and evening. In the afternoon, I go home, have lunch and then take a short nap before going back to the shop. But lately I've have begun to hate the afternoon naps. Even though I feel drowsy as hell, I'm afraid to even close my eyes. It makes my entire day miserable.'

'What happens?' Sarbajeet prodded, understanding his hesitation.

'Very well. So the thing is, these past few weeks I keep being abruptly woken up from my nap, but no matter what I do, I cannot move. Then I feel this heavy weight on my chest, and I see the demon. It sits on my chest. Its weight is so immense that I cannot do anything. It suffocates me and pins me down, and I can't move my arms or legs. I can't even turn my head. It hypnotizes me to keep looking at its ugly face. Mind it, I am conscious. I am awake. I want to get up and sit up, but I can't. I see my wife moving around, doing her work, but she can't see me. I want to scream and call out to her, but no word leaves my mouth. It's difficult to even breathe. In fact, when this happened the first time, I thought I was dead.'

Sarbajeet exchanged a look of understanding with his partner Pooja. Then he leaned forward and asked, 'So you really see the creature. Does it come to you otherwise, I mean, apart from the times when you nap? Does it influence you in any other way?'

'Of course!' Naved said. 'What else will you call it then, this hangover I have for the rest of the day? I feel dark inside, very dark and negative, and so depressed that I can't concentrate on anything. I've seen him, yes, dark and ugly. His face is menacing and full of anger. He's happy that he has this kind of hold on me. I'm sure... I'm sure he'll kill me one day.'

After Naved left, Sarbajeet had a long discussion with Pooja about his issue. What was throwing them off was his very vivid description of the demonic figure. Sarbajeet was particularly fascinated. His knowledge of demonology made him suspect that there was probably more to it than met the eye.

It was decided that they would supervise Naved's next afternoon nap. Naved agreed to have a camera set up in his room to record his nap. This went on for a few afternoons without anything odd showing up, and then a week later he returned to the office with his laptop. He had had another attack and was too afraid to watch the recording of it alone.

The three of them watched the recording together. It lasted an hour and forty minutes, which corresponded to the duration of his nap. Every detail was carefully observed.

For the first 30 minutes, Naved's sleep was undisturbed. He was relaxed, and snored lightly and rhythmically. Then the disturbance began. His eyes began to flutter, slowly at first and then faster. Then for about two minutes they fluttered so rapidly that you could see the whites of his eyes. Naved was scared to see himself this way, but Sarbajeet said, 'This is normal. It happens to most of us in deep sleep. This is your dream phase, known as rapid eye movement, REM. Nothing to worry about.'

His eyelids relaxed. The snoring resumed its rhythmic pattern. This continued for several more minutes, during which he was completely relaxed. Then he entered the REM phase again, and this time it wasn't so gentle as before. His eyelids began to flutter again, more rapidly now, and a faint line of sweat ran down his temple. His breathing turned heavy. His toes curled, and his fingers throbbed as if struggling to move.

'Here,' Naved said as he saw the recording. 'I had the attack here. Look!'

He pointed to his chest in the video. There was nothing there, but it was clear that he felt as if something was pinning him down. His entire upper body was rigid. His neck was stretched out, and his head was turned upwards at an odd angle. His mouth was closed, but his jaws were clearly clenched. Meanwhile, his eyes continued to flutter in the same violent fashion.

'He was sitting on my chest. Look! Look at my neck. He tried to strangle me,' Naved said, stricken with a horror that only he could experience.

'But there's nothing there,' Pooja remarked.

They continued to watch this painful segment of the video, which lasted about three minutes. Then Naved abruptly gasped and woke up. His eyes opened, and his arm made a rapid movement as if he was suddenly free of a tight hold. He sat up in bed, his shirt soaked in sweat.

'What do you say now?' Naved asked.

Sarbajeet took a minute to gather his thoughts and then said, 'Tell me, Naved, when you saw the video, did you see the demon in it?'

'No. But he was there!'

'Did you see him? Or perceive any sign of him?'

Naved shook his head.

'This is not demonic possession, unlike what you think,' Sarbajeet said.

'So you mean to say demonic possessions don't happen at all?'

'They do, but not like this. What you suffer from, dear Naved, is a condition known as sleep paralysis. And I can understand why you might feel that this condition is a demonic haunting.'

Following this pronouncement, Sarbajeet and Pooja took turns to explain to Naved what sleep paralysis was, and why he should not worry about it so much since there are ways to overcome this very common but rarely spoken-of condition.

Sleep Paralysis

Sleep paralysis is a condition where an individual is aware of the surroundings but is unable to interact with them, in the phase when they are falling asleep or waking up.

Affecting millions of people around the globe on a recurrent basis, sleep paralysis has attracted much research. Several explanations for the various symptoms have been put forward (some even conclusively proven), including those where individuals have reported seeing a demon-like creature while in the throes of a sleep paralytic attack. Let's look at an explanation from different angles and start where it all begins—with the earliest evidence thereof in mythology and folklore.

Sleep Paralysis in Mythology

Sleep paralysis is quite an ancient phenomenon, recorded from the earliest stages of human evolution. As such, it finds mention in the mythologies of cultures across the world. One of the most common terms to describe sleep paralysis is the 'old hag syndrome'. The old hag or night hag was believed to be a supernatural entity who would visit people when they were asleep and, if they suddenly tried to wake up, she would immobilize them so that they would not be able to catch her. Most times, she would immobilize them by sitting on their chest, which fits in quite well with the symptoms of sleep paralysis. This demonic old hag was variously named. In Greek mythology, she was called Maron, while in Sanskrit mythology, its gender is male, and is mentioned as Mara. In fact, this is where the word 'nightmare' originates from.

Mentions of the old hag are found in European folklore where they have developed into local legends. In Scandinavian mythology, there is a mare, a demonic creature, who sits on the chests of sleeping people and crushes their ribcages. The people of Fiji have another interesting take on the old hag. They believe that the spirits of dead relatives sometimes visit you when you are asleep, and sit on your chest to make you do their unfinished business. This 'business' is often of a dubious, even criminal, nature. The only way to get out of this is to curse the dead relative's spirit till it leaves.

A common Turkish belief is that sleep paralysis is caused by a djinn who sits on your chest while you sleep. The djinn is small in size but incredibly heavy. To get rid of the djinn, one has to try and reach the large hat that he wears on his head. It is believed that if the sleeping person manages to get that hat, the djinn will become their slave.

It is noteworthy that in both the Fijian and Turkish traditions, the person is required to actively do something to get rid of the 'demon'—either cursing or trying to take the hat. Both activities require energy and movement, which is exactly what is needed for the person to overcome a bout of sleep paralysis. It's wonderful how myths from around the world often contains kernels of reality, and show us the right thing to do without being too overt.

There are prominent mentions of the old hag in almost all Indian lore. In parts of Bengal and what is now Bangladesh, people speak of the *Boba*—a slimy, dark creature that emerges from the cover of darkness, and pins you down by sitting on your chest, leaving you speechless. In fact, the word 'boba' translates to 'dumb' or 'speechless'. Again, something can be done to ward off the Boba. If the sufferer confesses his or her recent sins, the Boba leaves the person and vanishes into the darkness.

Kashmiris believe in a spiritual presence known as *Pasikdar*. They believe that there is a Pasikdar in every house, who lies hidden throughout the day and cannot be seen. It does not come out if the house is well managed, both in terms of hygiene and religious adherence. But if the people living in the house do not keep the house clean, or fail to follow their rituals, then the Pasikdar comes out and tries to suffocate the family in their sleep.

The most popular Western legend around sleep paralysis is that of the incubus. The incubus is a male creature that is believed to visit people in their sleep, and have sex with them. The incubus sits on the sleeping person without waking them, and proceeds to do the deed. The sleeping person experiences this as a vivid erotic dream. When its deed is done, the incubus slips away, unseen. The person wakes up later to experience extreme fatigue and a definite sense that they have been violated during the night. The experience leaves the person with a bad hangover-like sensation in its wake. Similar to the incubus is the succubus, its female counterpart, which is also believed to act in a similar fashion but on the opposite gender.

Paranormal Beliefs on Sleep Paralysis

Different paranormal investigators have different theories on sleep paralysis, and they range from strictly scientific to strictly supernatural ones, and cover everything in between. Those who believe that sleep paralysis is indeed caused by a demonic creature attribute it to the negative energy radiated by the sufferer, which can be caused by certain internal factors such as depression, trauma, sickness, or exhaustion. It is their belief that this negative energy attracts supernatural elements such as demons which might cause sleep paralysis.

However, Sarbajeet and Pooja both rubbish this notion. After studying over 40 cases of sleep paralysis and conducting extensive research on the issue, they conclude that the reason for sleep paralysis is purely scientific. It is an entirely biological phenomenon that can be controlled and even got rid of by a change in lifestyle.

Let me share my own experience with sleep paralysis.

Soon after my post-graduation in 1998, I started a coaching institute. As the number of students grew, work became hectic, and I had to have batches throughout the day. For lunch, I'd be able to barely squeeze an hour and a half in the afternoons, during which I'd also include a brief shut-eye on a cot in the balcony of my room. It was at this time that my sleep paralysis bouts began.

At first, they were just stray incidents of feeling tethered to the cot, then they graduated to the sense of being bound by iron shackles on my hands and feet. I would be consciously awake and aware of my surroundings but my eyes would be shut and I'd be completely immobile, unable to even move a finger.

This was such a defeating, debilitating feeling that, just like Naved, I'd feel I have died.

I could see the people in my house even with my closed eyes and I'd try to shout to make them aware of my condition, but I had no voice.

This was the nineteen nineties, mind, and we had no resources to research or even know what sleep paralysis was. The condition would leave me sapped of all energy and thoroughly devoid of any enthusiasm for any activity afterwards.

And then it only became worse.

During the spells, I began to see a figure. A dark, formless entity sitting on my chest, grinding my ribs with its heavy weight, leering at me with its white, white eyes. I was in my twenties, and I totally believed this was the devil who had come to take me, and one day he would. I lived in abject terror, so much that I tried not to sleep at all.

One afternoon, I had the most terrifying experience of my life.

I had an episode of sleep paralysis. The dark entity had appeared, and I was smothered by its weight. Feeling crushed and totally defeated, I could do nothing else but lay still. Then something snapped inside me. I felt a release, like I had suddenly turned lighter. The next instant, I began to float up in the air. It was terrifying; I was going against gravity. Like I were nothing, I drifted up, towards the cracked ceiling, and there I stuck, like a balloon filled with helium. From there, I turned to look down, and—it gives me chills even as I write this—I could see *myself* down there on the cot with the dark being sitting on my chest.

It lasted for a few seconds, and then there was a white flash. It blinded me and then I was there again, back on the cot, back in my body, and I was awake.

This incident shook me so much that I tried to find out what was going wrong with me. I hit the best resource we had at that time, books, and I discovered the term 'sleep paralysis'.

It has been so many years that I forgot the name of the book, but I remember very well how it was explained scientifically. In layperson's terms: *the mind is awake but the body is not.* I realized what was going wrong. I was working too hard. My body was so fatigued that it had no strength to respond to my brain's attempts to wake me up. It was not heeding my biological alarm that was trying to tell me, 'Neil, wake up, it's time to go to your classes and teach your students.' In a way, it was my body rebelling against me.

When I made my workload lighter by reducing the size of my batches and employing more staff, my spells of sleep paralysis reduced, and then completely stopped. They returned in my forties a couple of times when I started writing horror, but I discovered that they were more of a psychological nature—my horror stories were replaying in my mind. Now, after taking up running and a lifestyle centred on fitness, I have found the perfect balance for my mentally challenging career as a horror writer, and I feel I am in the best phase of my life.

And yet, I have no real explanation for the dark figure that would sit on my chest, or the out of body experience of floating up in the air. On some lonely nights, I am impinged by the worry that the entity would return and this time, he'd claim me.

Scientific Theories to Explain Sleep Paralysis

Human sleep can be divided into four stages: Stage 1 non-REM sleep, Stage 2 non-REM sleep, Stage 3 non-REM sleep, and REM sleep. In the three non-REM stages, the person gradually falls deeper and deeper into a relaxed state of sleep, with stage 3 being the deep sleep stage from which it is difficult to rouse the individual. During this phase, the person's muscle tone is relaxed, and the heartbeat and brain functions slow down to the minimum requirement. It is worth noting that the person's motor abilities grind to an almost complete halt at this stage, i.e. their voluntary muscles are locked down. A common explanation for this is that the body tries to prevent the person from acting out the dreams, which could lead to injury.

The fourth stage of sleep is what requires our attention. This is REM sleep, the rapid eye movement stage. During this stage, the person enters a state of dreaming. This can be externally observed by the fluttering of the person's eyes and a few other symptoms such as heavier breathing, and at times, an increased pulse rate. Attacks of sleep paralysis occur during this phase.

Essentially, at the REM stage, the person is trying

to wake up. However, due to a dissonance in the REM stage and the time of waking, the person may still be in a dream-like state where the body is locked down while they are partially awake. The individual might be able to see and hear what's happening around them because these senses have woken up, but the voluntary muscles may still be locked, so the person is unable to move their arms and limbs. This is consistent with the studies done on people who have reported sleep paralysis, because most of these cases occurred when the individual is trying to wake up.

There is also an explanation for the demonic presence that most people report when they describe their sleep paralytic attacks. The demon might be nothing more than a hallucination. This occurs due to specific neural triggers that the person goes through when trying to wake up. The demonic presence is usually described as sitting on the person's chest and pinning them down, which is consistent with the fact that the person feels heaviness in the chest because their muscles are in a state of lockdown.

Another Interesting Case

Tanuj was a 15-year-old college-goer when he had for the first time what turned out to be one of the most hair-raising and recurrent experiences of his life. He was living in an all-boys hostel at the time without much adult supervision, and took to various vices. Smoking and consuming alcohol became almost a routine thing. In addition, he had a girlfriend back home which led to long chats till late in the night. Understandably, his routine was all haywire.

He recounts his experience thus, 'My dorm was on the fourth floor and my bed was adjacent to a large glass window that opened into the wilderness. Every night I fell asleep feeling a bit of uneasiness due to my messy daily schedule. Then, one night, I had a strange feeling. It appeared to be a dream, at first but it was so vivid. I heard footsteps outside and the crunch of dried leaves. The footsteps became louder and I could hear them as they climbed the stairs and made their way into my room and very close to my bed. But then I realized that I couldn't move. I had the sense that someone was very close to me, bending down and blowing air into my ear, but no matter how hard I tried, I couldn't even move a finger. This excruciating feeling lasted for a while, and then I suddenly felt as if I was free of whatever was holding me down. I sat up in bed and looked around—there was nothing there.

'This began to happen frequently. Some nights it happened twice or thrice. Sometimes I could even see the figure creeping up on me in my peripheral vision. I could hear their voice screaming or clapping in my ear. It was terrifying.'

When asked about his current condition (he is now 25), Tanuj says, 'I did some research on the condition and then I stumbled upon this particular discussion on the internet about 'sleep paralysis'. I knew that this was my condition. I understood that what I was experiencing was not any kind of ghostly or demonic presence, but a condition which was specifically brought on by my lifestyle. Later, as my life gained more stability and my sleep patterns became regular, I experienced these terrifying episodes less and less often. I still have them when my lifestyle undergoes any alteration, but now I know what it is. In fact, I am now fully conscious during these attacks even if I can't move, and I tell myself that this is just a trick of the nerves. It will pass. I try to move my fingers slowly. This helps me snap out of my condition.'

Tanuj's example is quite illuminating because it shows how vivid the hallucinations of sleep paralysis can be. It is understandable why people have attributed these attacks to ghosts and demons for centuries. It also shows how a few healthy lifestyle adjustments can reduce both the intensity and frequency of these attacks to a point when they no longer occur at all.

Tips to Avoid Sleep Paralysis Attacks

Even though the exact cause of sleep paralysis is not yet known, there are some ways by which these episodes could be avoided[7].

1. It has been observed that most sleep paralysis episodes occur when the person is lying on their back. For chronic sufferers, it is advised that they avoid sleeping on their backs. They can sleep on one side of the body, either right or left.
2. A regular sleep schedule is important. Sleep paralysis episodes happen mostly when the sleep schedule is disturbed. Even if our lifestyle does not permit a regular

[7]Note that this isn't medical advice, but observations from the experiences of multiple people who suffer from sleep paralysis (including myself). For chronic cases, seeking medical help is highly advised.

sleep schedule, it will help if we make some efforts in this regard.

3. Do not go to sleep immediately after heavy physical exercise. Let your body cool down to a state of relaxation before heading to bed.
4. Keep your mind free of distractions for at least an hour before going to sleep, especially if you are a regular sufferer. This means no social media. It is also necessary to keep the phone away from you when you sleep.
5. Avoid stimulants such as alcohol, caffeine and tobacco, especially at night before going to sleep.
6. If you experience sleep paralysis too often, you might want to consider light meditation. This will relax your neural pathways and ensure a more wholesome sleep experience.

For someone going through an episode of sleep paralysis, the experience can be quite discomforting. To cope with this, the first thing that the sufferer should consciously understand is that this is not the handiwork of a supernatural entity. It is simply the body trapped in a state of lockdown, and one can snap out of it. The person must slowly try to move their extremities, i.e. the toes and fingers first. As the episode lasts only a few minutes at the most, the torment will soon pass. Keeping this in mind, one can avoid the gloomy feeling that follows sleep paralysis.

LIVES LEFT BEHIND

Past-Life Regression

Our body is just a vehicle for us while we are here. It is our soul and our spirit that last forever.

—Dr Brian Weiss

It was the twilight hour on an uncharacteristically cold night in October. In Navi Mumbai, the office of PAIRS was filled with an uneasy silence. At first glance, the case that was brought to them seemed completely out of place. But as the discussion progressed and more facts unfolded, an entirely new perspective began to emerge.

Sitting across the table from them was a 25-year-old corporate worker named Subhash. Subhash had moved to Mumbai from Chhattisgarh a year ago, and was now settled in his new job. In Mumbai, he lived alone. The reason for his visit was not something that paranormal investigators often hear. 'I have a constant pain in my back,' he said. 'I have been to about twenty doctors in various cities and towns. They all say there's nothing wrong with me. But only I know how terrible the pain is, especially at night.'

While the duo waited for him to say more, Subhash

continued, 'A friend of mine suggested that the reason could be something non-medical…er…something beyond the natural. He says I might be possessed. To tell you the truth, I don't believe in such stuff, but it has been months without a solution, so I thought, "Why not?"'

Pooja noticed something about the man that probably he himself had not seen yet. At least, he hadn't mentioned it. Subhash wasn't sitting upright. There was a pronounced droop in his shoulders. She asked, 'Don't mind me asking so directly, but do you always sit like this, with a slouch?'

Subhash looked at his reflection in the glass window across him. He noticed his slouch and seemed to only register it at that moment. He tried to correct his posture, but the moment he tried that, he made an expression of great pain.

'Okay, okay, all right,' said Pooja. 'Please wait here. We will have a discussion and then come back to you.' With that, Pooja left the room with Sarbajeet. For the next ten minutes, they discussed the case in the other room. A decision was made, and they returned to the office. Pooja said, 'All right, Subhash, this is what we have decided. If your pain has no medical cause, then the cause may lie somewhere in your past. We can try to put you through regression therapy and see if anything comes up.'

The term visibly unnerved the man. 'What is that? I have never heard of such a thing.'

Pooja reassured him. 'You have nothing to worry about. All I'm going to do is to put you in a completely relaxed state, and then ask you a series of questions. I will try to find the cause of your agony and once we know it, we will think of a cure. Do you want to try it?'

Subhash wasn't convinced. He asked Pooja about everything that the therapy would entail and left the office with a cloud of apprehension hanging over his head. Three days later, he was back in the office. It was the same twilight hour. 'I can't take it anymore,' he said. 'Please go ahead with the therapy.'

Arrangements were made immediately. The office room was prepared for the therapy. All sounds and distractions were turned off and the curtains were drawn. Subhash was made to take off his shoes and socks, roll up his sleeves, take off his belt, and sit comfortably in a reclining chair. The lights were dimmed and then Pooja began talking to him in a soft voice.

'I am going to take you on a journey, Subhash,' she said. 'Relax completely and clear your mind. You are going into your memories, into your past. Unwind as much as you can. Breathe. You are in a safe place. You will see many things you have forgotten about yourself. We just want to try to see when the pain originated. Were you hurt at some point and then forgot about it?'

After a few minutes of talking in such a soothing fashion, Pooja paused and then asked, 'Can you hear me, Subhash?'

Subhash made a grunting sound. His eyes were half-closed; he seemed to be wavering between wakefulness and sleep. Pooja let him be there for ten minutes, occasionally telling him, in a soothing voice, to relax and let himself go.

When Subhash seemed to have entered a state of complete relaxation, Pooja knew he was ready. Softly, she said, 'Subhash, look at your feet now. What do you see?'

Subhash mumbled as if he was talking in his sleep.

Pooja leaned closer to him, and heard, 'I see…a ground. I am on a large open ground.'

'Yes, go on,' Pooja nudged him.

'I am wearing shoes of leather that are up to my knees.'

Pooja and Sarbajeet exchanged a look. Initially they thought that Subhash had been hurt at some point and the regression would make him see it. But what was happening was beyond their expectations. The man had regressed into another life.

Containing her excitement, Pooja asked him, 'Subhash, can you see where you are?'

Subhash mumbled, 'It's an open ground. Wait…I am looking around me now. No, I am not alone. There are many people around me. They are all men. They are all dressed like me. I have something in my hand. I see it now. It's a sword…'

Pooja breathed heavily. 'Sword? Are you describing a battlefield?'

'Yes, that's what this is. It's a battlefield.'

'Go on, Subhash. Do you know what year it is?'

'It is 1562.'

Pooja did not ask how he knew. Regressed people gain an awareness of their surroundings just by virtue of being in that location and time.

'What else is happening? Describe it in detail, Subhash,' Pooja said.

Subhash fell silent. His eyes half-closed, he was reliving something hidden in the deepest recesses of his memory. Every now and then, his fingers twitched in an involuntary motion. He had an expression as if he was disturbed by whatever he was seeing.

'What do you see, Subhash?'

Then he spoke as if with great effort. 'A fight is going on. I am in the middle of it.' He paused again and his face contorted into a grimace. 'Oh no...' he exclaimed and raised his arm.

Sarbajeet moved in to hold him, but Pooja signalled to him to let him go on. 'Keep talking, Subhash. What's happening?' Pooja asked.

Even as they looked at Subhash, his face contorted into a grimace, as if he were undergoing an immense degree of pain.

'Talk to us, Subhash,' Pooja prodded. 'What's happening?'

'Someone...a sword...behind my back...'

'Who is it, Subhash?'

'An enemy soldier...I am falling...so much blood...'

Though Sarbajeet was worried at this point, Pooja took the bold decision of allowing the regression to go on. 'Subhash, can you see anything else?' she asked.

'I am on my knees...wait, oh, wait...I can see his face.'

'Go on...'

'Oh no...' Subhash said and then his hands began to shiver.

Pooja took his trembling hands in her own. 'What's it, Subhash?'

'I see his face...'

'Yes. And?'

'He's my father. The enemy soldier is my father.'

Pooja and Sarbajeet looked at each other, agape, not knowing what to say.

'My father stabbed me in my back,' Subhash went on.

'Snap him out of it, Pooja,' Sarbajeet said.

Pooja then said in a firmer voice, 'Subhash, you are not in that place. You are here, in our office. I am Pooja. You must leave that place and come back to us.'

No sooner were those words spoken than Subhash relaxed. He stopped moving and collapsed on the chair and lay still for several moments. Pooja exhorted him to open his eyes after a couple of minutes. Subhash did so and blinked to see his surroundings.

'I am sorry that was so intense,' Pooja said after several minutes had passed. 'You did not just regress into the past in this life, but into one of your past lives.'

'It was so intense as if I was really there, like it was really happening to me,' Subhash said, finding his breath, 'and now I know so much. I know what causes me the pain, and why my relationship with my father is so strained.'

Pooja nodded. 'Our past lives sometimes leave imprints on our present ones.'

A cold chill swept through the room as Pooja uttered those words.

Subhash took in the words slowly and then said, 'Since my earliest years, I have been close to my mother but have never gelled with my father. I have no shame in admitting that I don't like him. I have always avoided him as much as possible.'

Pooja merely nodded, allowing him to vent out his feelings, and more than that, to analyse what he had just experienced.

Then Pooja said, 'Subhash, I'll only tell you one thing. Whatever a man does in a past life should not impede their present life. You must talk to your father again.'

Subhash heeded the advice, though it was tough for him. Over time, he realized that his father was a different person in this birth. He had no recollection of his past life, and moreover, he loved Subhash abundantly. The realization worked as a bridge between them, and with the constant guidance of Pooja and Sarbajeet, Subhash reconciled with his father.

Past-Life Regression

Past-life regression is the technique by which a person is put under hypnosis and made to recall memories of a past life or incarnation.

Past-life regression or PLR has always been a hot topic of discussion in the world of parapsychology. Though it does not entail ghosts, it has to do with what a person was in their past life, which indirectly speaks of lives before birth and after death. It has a special place in spiritualism too, which believes that people are shaped by what they were in their past lives, and their present lives are but a culmination of their life's journey which has brought them up to this point.

PLR practitioners believe in the concept of reincarnation and the existence of a soul. When the soul is reborn, the memories that are imprinted on the soul from the past life are transferred into the new body, or specifically, the brain. However, these memories stay suppressed in the person. These past-life memories may be more profound up to the age of five years, but they are gradually suppressed as the child learns new things in the present life. Almost all of us lose all recollection of our past lives once we cross the age of five. However, in certain scenarios, these memories can come to the fore. Proponents of PLR believe that the phenomena termed as 'déjà vu' (the feeling that something has happened before), 'presque vu' (the strong feeling that something similar to a present activity has happened before), and 'déjà entendu' (the feeling that a sound has been heard before), all have their roots in past-life memories.

The Process of Past-Life Regression Therapies

The basic reason why most people go for PLR is to know the cause of something that is troubling them in their present life. These issues can be either physical or mental, but there are no visible reasons for their existence. It could be a mystery ailment whose symptoms are profound, but doesn't appear to have a cause, such as in the case of Subhash, or it could be an underlying psychological issue of unknown origin.

In Pooja Vijay's experience, PLR has worked in the case of many of her clients. Once the root cause is identified, which is a revival of a memory of a past life, the issue happens to resolve itself. To put her clients through regression, Pooja follows a 7-step technique.

Pooja issues a disclaimer to anyone who reads the following points. 'These are points that I use for my regression therapies and I have learnt them from my father. I went through a lot of training before I could professionally conduct such sessions. Although I share my methods here, I need to point out that this is by no means a do-it-yourself guide. It is possible to put the subject to serious harm if such a therapy is performed by a non-professional.'

Step 1: Interview

The therapy opens with a detailed interview. It is a way of understanding the person, their fears, their belief systems, and their general disposition towards things in their present life. Interview questions are specifically designed to analyse if there are any recurring patterns.

Step 2: Identifying the Core Issue

The therapist will try to find out as much as possible about the problem or issue that the person faces, and if that is the reason for them to opt to undergo a PLR session. This enables the therapist to know what needs to be addressed. Then the therapist decides the procedure that the PLR session will follow.

Step 3: Induction

This is where the regression actually begins. The person is made to relax as much as possible. Using comforting verbal instructions, an attempt is made to hypnotically transport the person back to their previous life. During this stage, the responses from the person tend to be quite confusing, as they might be glancing into several past lives at once. If hypnosis does not work, certain non-hypnotic methods can also be used.

Step 4: Locating the Lifetime

The therapist asks increasingly specific questions to help

the person determine the exact lifetime where the issue originated. This is the most challenging part of the PLR session, and can take a considerable amount of time. This is also the phase where most PLR sessions abruptly end in failure.

Step 5: Journeying the Lifetime

If successful, the therapist further sharpens their questions to guide the person to that exact moment in their past life where the issue originated. This could be the inciting incident that causes the pain or anguish in the present life. The questions asked will be about the person's gender, family circumstances, the time in which they lived, the social conditions, and such others. Since a significant number of questions are to be asked in this phase, this is the most time-consuming of all phases. It is also the most delicate, as a single wrong or insensitive question might pull the person out of the phase.

Step 6: Healing and Integration

Once the issue is located, the therapist uses verbal approaches to repair the problems in that lifetime, if possible. This is the suggestive phase of the therapy, where a suggestion is made that the person's issue is resolved in the past life, which implies that it would no longer have any repercussions in their present life.

Step 7: Closure

All PLR sessions must be properly concluded, and the person brought back into the present. If this is not done, the person might stay in a state of limbo, because a part of their brain will continue to think of the past life. Closure also signifies that the issue the person faces has been resolved.

One might not be immediately aware whether a PLR therapy is successful or not. Once the therapy is completed, the person is asked to closely monitor the issue they were suffering from and see if it persists. Pooja has found that in most cases, the awareness of the cause of the issue works in a therapeutic manner. Resolving underlying emotions goes a long way in rectifying certain problems that stump even conventional medical practitioners.

Criticism of Past-life Regression Therapy

Past-life regression methods have come under their fair share of criticism. The theory of PLR depends on a person's belief in past lives and rebirth, and the existence of an immortal soul, which are concepts that are still not proven scientifically. Medical science largely discredits PLR's ability to impart any therapeutic benefit, or even its scientific soundness, for that matter.

The description of past-life memories has also been discredited by critics. The explanation is that these memories are generated during therapy, either through suggestive questioning by the therapist, or the imagination of the person on the basis of an association with their life's experiences. In certain experiments, the memories described by persons undergoing PLR directly or indirectly originate in components of their present life, such as the books they read, movies they watched, or places they visited. In some cases, people's descriptions of their past lives contain historically inaccurate information as they might have come across that inaccurate information in a book or a movie. Critics say that the ambience created during a PLR session and the line of questioning make the imagination so powerful that the brain conditions itself to think that this might have happened at some point in the past. Such a phenomenon where the subconscious mind creates its own narratives due to suggestion and imagination and thinks that they are real is called as cryptoamnesia, which is a known psychological condition.

Pooja is aware of such criticism. She has full faith in the practice, though, which stems from her belief in the Metaphysical Theory of Survival Hypothesis, which states that the human consciousness survives physical death. This theory has neither been proved nor disproved, but it might be the answer to the mystery that surrounds PLR. Put simply, the subconscious mind is a bank for all the imprints and memories of all the past lives of a human being. If there is a past life, which Pooja does not doubt, there won't be just one but several of them, and each would leave behind several impressions on the soul's memory. A deep analysis of this concept, supported by experiments on numerous people, was conducted by Dr Brian Weiss, the author of the book *Many Lives, Many Masters.*

Apart from this, Pooja's belief in PLR has a more practical explanation. In her experience, she has seen several people like Subhash who were cured of physical problems that conventional medicine could not address. Apart from the dissolution of causeless physical pains, there have also been a vast number of cases where she has managed to correct emotional trauma in people's present lives after discovering that the root cause of discordant relationships lay in some unsavoury connection with the person in a past life.

However, the strongest response to the criticism around PLR comes from the hundreds of cases around the world where children as young as four years old have managed to correctly recall a past life. These narratives are chilling to the core. The case of Shanti Devi from Delhi attracted great fame, so much so that a special committee was set up by the Indian government to establish her claims. Here are the details of her case.

When Shanti Devi was four, she began to say that her house was somewhere in Mathura, which was 150 km away from her present home. She mentioned that she was a married woman and her husband's name was Kedar Nath. The more chilling fact was that she suddenly started using words that were in the dialect of Mathura, and were not used in her hometown. Her parents tried to put an end to these conversations, but when she turned six, she mentioned her 'memories' to her school headmaster. Intrigued, the headmaster conducted some inquiries in Mathura and found out that there was indeed a man named Kedar Nath fitting the description given by Shanti Devi, and he lived in a similar house. This Kedar Nath had lost his wife Lugdi Devi just ten days after she gave birth to their child. Kedar Nath was contacted, and he came to meet Shanti Devi, but he came with the alias of his younger brother and gave a different name. Shanti Devi, however, immediately recognized him as her husband from her past life and fell at his feet.

Shanti Devi's case, which occurred in the 1930s, drew the world's attention towards the concept of reincarnation.

Medical science, despite its theories and arguments to the contrary, failed to offer any scientific explanation for her case and it remains a mystery to this day. There are hundreds of such cases worldwide, where science is unable to apply any of the known forms of reasoning. And that is what keeps the belief of the PLR therapists alive in their form of practice.

Pooja shared another story of a young girl's regression, which is unique because of the intricate web of relationships that it weaves. This story indicates that our souls may also be connected to other souls, such as those of our relatives and friends, who travel with us across lifetimes.

Tina was in the Third Year of her B.Sc. course, and due for her final examinations. She was brought to the PAIRS office by her mother Alka. Mother and daughter had always had interpersonal problems, which were further complicated by the arrival of a man in Tina's life. The man was Lilesh, whom she had met during an interview. The bond between Tina and Lilesh had grown strong in a short period of time, but Alka did not share her admiration for him. In fact, the very mention of his name put her on the edge.

Matters had become strained between the mother-daughter duo. Alka had gone to the extent of tracking her phone, calling up her friends, and even restraining her from leaving the house. Tina was contemplating leaving the house, as this was also affecting her studies.

The curious part was that both knew they could mend their relationship, and had even tried to do so, but eventually gave up, and were at loggerheads again. It was as if some unknown emotional issue was pulling them apart.

Finally, a friend of the family recommended that they try regression therapy. He had undergone the procedure and found it beneficial. After a long discussion, Alka and Tina decided to give it a shot to see if there was something else causing this problem that they were unable to understand.

Tina came prepared to undergo regression therapy. Pooja conducted the preliminary interview, and tried to understand the issue as clearly as possible. Tina was then put through the phase of induction.

However, despite her preparedness, Tina wasn't ready for the shocking revelations that came up. I will summarize the revelations here.

Tina easily regressed and quickly entered a hypnotic state, and began to describe the new world that she was seeing around her. She saw herself as a princess in a small kingdom in Belgium, but she could not specify the year. In that life, she had a doting father. She spoke of her love interest, a man named Leon, whom she was enamoured with. During the induction, she took a lot of time to describe Leon's appearance—he was a strikingly handsome man with blond hair.

Now came the shocking part of her revelation. As she saw the faces of the people around her closely, she saw that her father in that life, the king of the land, was none other than Lilesh, her present-day boyfriend. If this wasn't scandalous enough, there was something else—her previous life's boyfriend Leon bore a striking resemblance to Alka, her mother in her current life.

This was more complicated than a Spanish telenovela! For the first time, Pooja found it difficult to keep track of the tangled lifelines across births. She had to keep writing details down in a notebook so as not to lose anything.

Pooja led Tina deeper into that life. Tina's descriptions were vivid. She spoke in a half-conscious state as if she were narrating a scene playing out in front of her. She spoke of the animosity between her father of the previous birth and Leon. Leon was a mere artist and did not earn well. The king did not want his daughter to marry such a man. To thwart their love, the king exiled Leon from the kingdom.

Tina's next description was a scene from the same birth, but many years later. She could see herself as a middle-aged woman working in the kitchen of a household. Her father had died but she hadn't become the next queen for a reason she could not explain. In this vision, she had a visitor. This visitor was Leon, who had grown older too. He was angry and told her that his life had been ruined by her father, and she hadn't stopped him. He had come to take revenge. Blinded in anger, he plunged a dagger into her stomach. As she lay dying, she saw Leon, overcome with grief, and he plunged the dagger into his own stomach.

When Tina came out of hypnosis, she was terribly exhausted and completely mentally drained. Pooja resolved the situation for her. Leon was now her mother. The rage of the previous life had left an imprint on her soul, which was now manifesting in this birth too. This explained the many altercations between mother and daughter. The entry of Lilesh into Tina's life, who was none other than the king, further aggravated matters.

As the threads of this past-life complication fell into place, Pooja spoke to both about how their issues were due to the imprints of their past lives. She counselled them to be aware of that, and endeavour not to let those memories affect their present relationship. With this knowledge, mother and daughter made peace with each other. A few years later, Tina married Lilesh, and they are now a happy family.

One incredible aspect of PLR therapies, which even its detractors attest to, is that it has a therapeutic effect on those who believe in the idea of a past life. It is akin to praying. Those who believe in God will experience the benefit of prayer. In a similar fashion, people who believe that they have had previous births will have more faith in regression, and believe that their problems might have traced their provenance to one of their past lives.

Although medical science stands divided on many concepts of rebirth and afterlife, including the existence of the soul, the many experiences of practitioners like Pooja Vijay who delve into people's past lives with such uncanny detail have sustained the general curiosity around the subject. Each case of regression presents a new layer to the existing knowledge, although an irrefutable proof of the truth behind past-life regression is still to be obtained.

IN CONCLUSION

As we come to the end of the chapters contained in the book, Sarbajeet and I take a moment to review and retrospect on what we have learnt in the process.

Our initial challenge was to choose ten subjects that we wished to talk about. While we sat down to do this daunting task, we realized how vastly the world of paranormal knowledge has grown over the years. No longer is it confined to just a few books found in the remote corners of dusty library shelves, but now there are thousands of podcasts, articles and blogs, blockbuster movies and web-series, and people coming out to speak about their own experiences. What was under wraps once upon a time, and even considered to be somewhat of a taboo subject, is now out in the open.

But with this came another challenge. We had to ensure that we put forth facts as accurately as possible. We had to sift the right knowledge from the tons of sensational content floating out there. This is why we delved into our own experiences, and of the people that we have come across, and corroborated them with research that is as scientific as it could be, given the nature of the subject.

Having said that, the paranormal world is still

considered to be within the domain of parascience (not true science), or science-adjacent, which is owing to the severe lack of evidence to confirm its theories. We maintain that nature of the paranormal domain as well, and put up a disclaimer here that nothing that's written in this book, or even in the paranormal world at large, must be taken as the gospel truth.

We have chosen ten topics which we have thoroughly analysed and presented for you. As the same time, there are hundreds of other established and accepted theories out there, and we continue to research on them and study them.

We hope that our paths cross again and we get the chance to talk to you about them as well.

Do talk about the book within your circles and drop us a review. It will mean a lot to us, and let us know that our work has hit the right chord. It will enable us to come back to you and shed more light on the darker recesses of the paranormal and supernatural worlds.

ACKNOWLEDGEMENTS

It is only when you sit down to write the 'Acknowledgements' page of a book that you realize the writing process isn't such a lonely journey after all. This especially rings true for our book, *Ghost Whispers.*

The person to set us on this journey was our literary agent, Suhail Mathur, of The Book Bakers. Not only did he introduce us to each other and be a part of conceptualizing *Ghost Whispers*, he also ensured that we got the best publishing platform possible. We owe Suhail our deepest gratitude; he is as much a part of this book as we are.

We have nothing but the deepest regard for our publishing team at Rupa Publications. It was a wonderful ride from pitching to publishing. We were supported by their guidance all along; they provided us with the fuel that kept this journey going.

A very special note of thanks is reserved for Pooja Vijay, eminent psychic, clairvoyant, and one-half of the founding team of PAIRS, for her generous insights and inputs that made this a better book. We extend this gratitude to all the other team members of PAIRS who shared their experiences with us and, in the process, enriched our storytelling.

No book can be created without the support and love

of our silent cheerleaders—our families. Over the three years that we worked on this book, there were personal challenges that tested our will power to complete the book. However, the steadfast support from our families ensured that we had the time, energy, and resources to make the book happen. If *Ghost Whispers* is in our readers' hands today, it is because of our families' unwavering support, and we thank them immensely for making our dream a reality.

The last word of thanks goes to all our readers, followers, friends and associates from the horror community, and everyone else who ever took a moment to contribute to the slightly unconventional work that we do.

You are all a part of the universe that is *Ghost Whispers*.

Thank you.
Neil D'Silva and Sarbajeet Mohanty